IN
IMAGE OF GOD

Male and Female
He Created Them

James Lindemann

James (Jim) Lindemann

Webpage: lindespirit.com
email: jim@lindespirit.com
Blog: CovenantMusings.lindespirit.com

©Copyright 2013: James Lindemann; All rights reserved
ISBN: 978-0-9916866-4-3
Photo Credit: Photos of The Sistine Chapel in the public domain
*1405

Other titles by the author:
COVENANT: The Blood Is The Life
Creation's Ballet for Jesus
Celebration! - Holy Communion: A Love Story
Living Waters - Baptism: From His Heart Through Ours
The Mystery of Suffering: Freedom From or Presence Within Suffering

RFL & Son, Publisher
541 33 Street South
Lethbridge, Alberta, Canada T1J 3V7

ISBN 978-0-9916866-4-3
90000
9 780991 686643

Flyleaf

It is obvious: the Creator is not visible to His creatures. The surprise is the realization that He could be, and He will be – after all, in eternity He will be as fully visible as He was to Isaiah, Ezekiel, Daniel and John in their visions. But in *this* universe He is nowhere to be observed. Or is He? If Creation wants to see its beloved Creator, where is it to look?

When humanity is created, it is given a unique reason for existing: it is to be in "the Image of God." The Creator's design is that here would be the *visible* reflection of Jehovah for the sake of the universe. What an honor, privilege, and responsibility! In a sense, the reality of God is to ride on the shoulders of human beings. There are things that the Lord will not do in any other way than through the hands of humankind.

Yet the Lord's blueprint is for a "binocular" view of Himself. As our two eyes give us the ability to recognize three dimensions around us, so also through the creation of "the man" and of "the woman," the combination has the opportunity to demonstrate a wonderful depth to God. This book explores what it means to be "the Image of God" and "the Soul-likeness of God" as demonstrated in the genders and the different tasks they are given. It is indeed necessary to investigate the stated purposes for their existence as a guide for the many discussions about the difference in roles – an aspect that is often neglected.

This is important because this is how the Creator becomes tangible and real – to themselves, to each other (particularly in marriage), to their children and to the whole *cosmos*.

The Author

The author, a pastor himself, is the recipient of perspectives, concerns and interests handed down from a long line of pastors in the Lutheran Church, hence his interest and background in such things as the Sacraments, the Covenant, and even the Star of Bethlehem. His Bible Study groups have also contributed greatly in developing these various themes, and now as retirement approaches, this is a good time to gather these thoughts into a more finished form.

Born and raised in New York City, he has come to also value life in smaller communities. With his deeply appreciated companion (his wife), their family bulges at the seams with four natural, two adopted, a variety of foster children, and now grandchildren – there is no end to the usually delightful competition for his attention. Perhaps in the coming years there may even be time to pursue his Master's interest in carpentry.

Table of Contents

Preface

This has been quite a project. It never was intended to be like this. I doubt that it would have gotten this far, had I known back then what I was in for.

It originally started as an article in response to a general request for Mother's Day articles on a Christian writers' webpage. That article never got published, but I put it on my weblog anyway. Then I decided to have a companion article on the weblog for Father's Day. Things didn't work out to get it done in time, but a couple of weeks later I set out to write it anyway. As I struggled with that article, I had realized that there were concepts that needed to be developed first or else there would be no firm footing for what was said in the article.

· I found myself centering on the concept of "the Image of God" as the theme basic to the existence of humankind, and as I paid attention to the words and the concepts that the Scriptural writers used, I became intrigued as to what was emerging. But by then, I reached an impasse: I was on the ninth blog post and needed to consolidate the various thoughts which had been expressed before I could go further. I needed to know where I had travelled, how consistent were the ideas, and how well did they fit together in the larger mosaic.

Thus began this book.

It has been quite a struggle to be as careful and as balanced, and especially as Biblical, as possible, particularly in order to avoid needless offense. God's Word will many times be offensive to our human nature, but it was that "needless" which I wanted to avoid.

So just how useful is "the Image of God" in understanding what humanity is about? What is there about "the male" and "the female" which makes *both* of them essential and yet individually unique within this "Image of God"? Each is specifically accented, each is separately created, each is given distinctive traits – why? What does this have to tell us about *who* they are and *what role* they have in demonstrating God to the Universe?

Literally by bits and drabs, various pieces took shape and fit together. Likely this topic will never be finished – it is not easily explained, and new understandings will surface. But what has been identified here, it is hoped, should start a thoughtful, hopefully *Biblical* dialogue.

I thank Jane Pollock for her sharp eye in disciplining my writing style and for keeping me honest and pastoral in my approach.

Jim Lindemann

February, 2014

Postscript:

Likely with varying degrees of accuracy, the Bible quote translations are mine, however there is a heavy dependence on:

The Interlinear Hebrew/Greek English Bible, 4 volumes
  Jay Green, ed., (Lafayette, IN: Associated Publishers and Authors, 1979)

As well as
The Online Bible computer program (http://www.onlinebible.net)
  Copyright in Canada
  by Larry Pierce
    (11 Holmwood St., Winterbourne, Ontario, N0B 2V0)

and particularly its modules for

  The Authorized or King James (1769) Version
  American King James Version
    Michael Peter (Stone) Engelbrite (True Grace Ministries)
  Placed into the public domain on November 8, 1999.

also its dictionary linking to *Strong's Concordance* numbers and to

R Laird Harris, *Theological Wordbook of the Old Testament* (Chicago: Moody Press, 1981)

Gerhard Kittel and Gerhard Friedrich, ed., *Theological Dictionary of the New Testament*, (Grand Rapids, MI: Wm. B. Eerdmans Publishing Co., 1966).

As well as the website: *http://interlinearbible.org*

1. The Hidden God Revealed

Yuri Gagarin

Yuri Gagarin was the first human to journey into outer space in the Vostok 1 spacecraft on April 12, 1961. Although he is reported to have observed that as he looked around at the edge of space he didn't see any God up there, likely that comment was actually made by Nikita Khrushchev. Either way, the problem with that conclusion is that they were looking for the evidence in the wrong place.

On Purpose?

It is obvious that God is hidden from our view.

But do you realize that this is *on purpose*?

He has no physical form by which we can recognize Him or see Him at work. Yet this is no accident – He planned it this way. He could have created an environment where He would be continually "in plain sight" – after all, on the Last Day, in "the new heaven and the new earth," there will be no trouble seeing Him in all His majesty.

Yet His choice has been a visible universe in which *He* would be invisible – why? Why has He created it this way? And how then are we – indeed all Creation – to catch any glimpses of Him?

Evidently He decided that right from the beginning "faith" would be required in human existence: "Now faith is ... the evidence of things not seen" [Hebrews 11:1]. Although unseen, the Creator would leave His footprints all over the Universe by which we could follow His activity:

For what can be known about God is plainly revealed to them – because *God* has revealed it to them! For from the creation of the world, the unseen things of God – especially His eternal power and divine nature – can be grasped and discerned by the things that are made, so they are without excuse.   Romans 1:19-20

Yet this is not enough. Yes, we can see His power and deity, but where might His creatures find His heart?

The Mirror

God said, "Let Us make man in Our Image, according to Our Likeness: and let them rule..."   Genesis 1:26

There is a way by which He can be "seen," although not directly. He designs a *mirror*, something that would reflect Him, something that would bear His "Image," something that would represent Him ("rule") before all Creation. He fashions a man from the dust of the ground and places into his nostrils His own Breath [Genesis 2:7].

Here is one of the great mysteries about the great Jehovah, something we would never have imagined. On one hand, He is supremely self-sufficient – He obviously needs no one to accomplish His will: He does not *need* angels and, for that matter, He really doesn't need *us* either. In fact, one might think that we humans too often get in His way and are too much of a bother and a liability to Him in what He wants to do.

Yet His *design* is to make *us* be *an essential partner* in what He does. He chooses to have humans be His physical representatives before Creation. Here is to be demonstrated those characteristics of the Creator that cannot be found in the stars and the planets, nor in the mountains and the seas, nor in the plants and the animals. Here is to be the Image of God's *heart*.

2

Think about it: what activity among humanity does God do that does not depend on using people? Whether it be clothing the naked, feeding the hungry, sheltering a stranger, touching the hurts of a person, taking ecological care of Creation, or whatever the task may be, people are the visible means by which these things are accomplished. He does not use angels for such activities (at least visibly), and He will not do it in any other way. In fact, we are so essential that when we will not do what He wants, it will not get done. Even in such crucial things as demonstrating forgiveness, portraying love, or making disciples of all nations – somewhere a person must be involved if these things are to going to happen.

It is not surprising then that His Commandments [Exodus 20:4; Leviticus 26:1; Deuteronomy 4:16] forbid any other image than this *living* one which *He* has placed upon the human – nothing else can match His design.

Binocular – Male and Female

So God created the man in His Image, in the Image of God created He him; male and female created He them.   Genesis 1:27

We have two eyes, almost identical, and not far apart. At first, one might think that this is unnecessary redundancy, yet the two eyes with that fixed distance between them make all the difference: they allow us to see in three dimensions. Now we become aware of depth and visual perspectives.

The male and the female provide a dual view of "the Image of God," and their differences together give depth and perspective to the great Jehovah. Truly, one eye by itself can do a very good job, and so also the male or the female individually can provide an important perception of God's activity in our world. However, when the two are put together, there is a richness and a fullness in added dimensions which just is not there individually.

The Full Image

Therefore, although invisible, God can now be seen – *if* the mirror is clear and clean. Unfortunately, the mirrors have become distorted and those glimpses of Him in the human are sometimes very obscure – "we see as in a mirror indistinctly" [I Corinthians 13:12].

What is surprising is that the Creator has not abandoned His plan! His design does not crumble nor is it negated by human rebellion. He chooses to make humans, although defective, nevertheless essential: they are still to be His way by which His Image is broadcast into this universe. Many things God simply does not do unless they are done by human hands. There still are boundless privilege and enormous responsibility held by those who are to be in "the Image of God."

On this basis, it is very important then to rediscover the blueprint upon which humanity was modeled.

2. The Image in the Mirror

The Design

One thing that the opening chapters of the Bible make clear is that the creation of humankind is no accident: there is personal attention to the man's formation; there is definite purpose in the making of the woman; there is a deliberate plan and goal for these new creatures.

Just like a picture can have the image of someone we love, Creation is to look at humans to find a recognizable "Image of God." We are marked with the stamp of God Himself – the breath of God. In us there are to be all kinds of clues – glimpses – of Him, glimpses especially of His heart.

The Challenge of Reconstruction

A picture was once taken of a light above the edge of a reflecting pool. The water was so calm that indeed the reflection was "the mirror image" of the light – you could describe exactly what the light looked like even if the original itself was not in the picture. Obviously the image could not tell you *everything* about the original, but you could at least identify its important visible characteristics, so that if you ever saw the original, you would immediately recognize it.

Now imagine a windy day. The surface of the water is rippled and chopped up. As a storm approaches, the image becomes less and less recognizable. Eventually the image becomes a mass of apparently unrelated glimmers and sparkles of light.

When humanity falls into sin, the effect is the same. The harsh wind of rebellion distorts and mars "the Image of God' in the great sea of humanity.

Oh, yes, there are indeed glimmers and sparkles of the Original to be seen, a bright spot here and there: acts of goodness, assorted wise sayings, genuine concern for people and the world, and more.

But the bright spots have far too many dark spots mixed with them – greed, selfishness, plunder, and destruction. So now when Creation looks to the representative of the Creator, it finds no clear Image. It is no wonder that nature simply reflects the chaos in the human heart. How then can "the Image of God" become restored?

"Peace, Be Still"

> Having dismissed the crowd, they took [Jesus] with them in the boat, also other boats were with Him. A storm of great wind came, the waves beating on the boat, so that it was already filled. But He was in the stern, sleeping on a pillow. They awoke Him and said to Him, "Teacher, don't You care that we perish?"
> Now awakened, He rebuked the wind, and said to the sea, "Silence! be muzzled!" The wind ceased and there was a great calm.
>
> Mark 4:36-39

Jesus commands the wind and sea and the effect is impressive. Using the reflecting pool example, when Jesus comes on the scene, the waters begin to quiet. Although we may wish for a dramatic change equal to the episode in Mark, God does things in His own time. Slowly, in His People, the blobs of light begin to coalesce. Gradually an Image begins to form. Certain characteristics become noticeable. Unfortunately it will take the Second Coming, when "Behold, I make all things new" [Revelation 21:5], before "the Image" becomes as clear as God's original design. However, the joy is that, in the meantime, "the Image" has its moments when there are recognizable features.

So what is this "Image of God" that is taking shape?

A Trinity

This topic can be helpful particularly in understanding not only how we can reflect "the Image of God," but also in how that Image has pronounced limitations. As well, it is a topic about God that we have great difficulty in describing to others. Yet we have overlooked a very real and present example: humans! It is with this dual purpose in mind that we contemplate the following.

"Spirit, Soul and Body"

> May the God of peace Himself sanctify you wholly; and may the whole of you, the Spirit and the Soul and the Body, be kept blameless at the coming of our Lord Jesus Christ.   I Thessalonians 5:23

Could it be that in reflecting God's Image, one of the characteristics which we show is that we are also a trinity? St Paul seems to indicate that very thing in I Thessalonians. Some have thought that "Spirit" and "Soul" are merely identical, but would Paul repeat the same concept unnecessarily? Perhaps in poetry there might be such repetition, but this is not poetry.

Furthermore, I Corinthians 15:44-46 indicates that the two terms are not identical. Paul sets up a contrast between what has been translated as the "natural" body and the "spiritual" body, the "natural" being the earth-oriented body and the "spiritual" being the heaven-oriented, fully born-again version which will reflect Jesus' resurrected body. The Greek word for "natural" is actually "Soul" in adjective form, for which English has no counterpart. But if we were to coin such an adjective form ("soulish"), then the passage would read like this:

> It is sown a "soulish" body, it is raised a spiritual body. If there is a "soulish" body, there is also a spiritual body. ... The spiritual did not come first, but the "soulish," and after that the spiritual.

If "Soul" and "Spirit" are identical, then the contrast Paul makes would be nonsense. However, if they are different, then just what are the differences between the human "Body, Soul and Spirit"?

The Body

Of the three, the Body is pretty obvious. That is what everyone can see. There really shouldn't be much to explain about that part of us.

The Soul and Life

The Soul, on the other hand, requires careful thought. In the Old Testament, the word for "Soul" is often simply translated as "Life" [for example, Leviticus 17:1] – in fact, "living" and "soul" are often linked together [for example, Genesis 2:7].

Here we embark on a mystery: a Body can be dead or alive – what constitutes the difference? What is this "Life"-principle, this Soul, all about?

Science insists that life is merely chemical reactions, but that just is not enough. A dead body also has chemical reactions occurring: in fact, the chemicals are doing what they would naturally do when left by themselves, but we call this "decay." No, there is something that compels these chemicals to go in a direction opposite from their natural tendency.

The story of Frankenstein promotes the idea that electricity must be that "spark of life"; after all, the body has tiny electric signals constantly running the different functions of the body. However this theory is problematic: whether plant or animal, anything struck by lightening demonstrates that simply adding raw energy tends to kill, cook, and char, but not impart life. It is hard to imagine how a lightening bolt, which in a fraction of a second has enough energy to power a major city for hours, could create something that runs on such minute surges of energy (which requires very sensitive equipment to recognize).

In modern technological terms, if lightening struck the earliest computers, which ran on far more power requirements than today's models, the result would still be that the delicate circuits would be fried. On the same order, the medical defibrillator's powerful surge of energy cannot bring life into a "flat line" heart – in fact, what it actually does is it causes the heart to *stop*, in the hope that a chaotic heartbeat will reboot to a normal rhythm. Only the very controlled small surge of electricity of the pacemaker may continue the life of a heart, yet even this will not resurrect a heart that has died.

Life (or the Soul) *uses* chemical reactions, it *uses* electricity in the body, but it is not defined by these things. Ultimately, we cannot tell what "Life" (or the Soul) *is*, however we can describe some of its effects: the Soul appears to have mental abilities, emotions, passions, and many other things which give each living creature its distinctive identity. But Soul is not unique to the human. Of the twelve times that the Hebrew for "living soul" first appears in the Bible [Genesis 1:20,21,24,30; 2:7,19; 9:10,12,15,16; Leviticus 11:10,46], only one refers to the human.

The Spirit

So if the "Soul" does not mark the difference between man and animal, what does? Genesis 2:7 tells us, "Jehovah God ... breathed into his nostrils the Breath of Life." No other creature is ever described as having this privilege, responsibility and burden. Adam bears the very Breath of God – it is something that comes from the center of God Himself; it is a remarkably intimate relationship with God, a relationship of "Spirit."

The spiritual side *may* be where creativity, ingenuity, artistry and the sense of beauty resides; however, it definitely houses prayer, spiritual insight, the awareness of the Holy Spirit's presence, and probably also such things as the conscience, sin-sickness, awareness of guilt, and other such traits.

This third part is the most difficult to describe because sin's most destructive effect has been in this area of the human's relationship with God. It is also the part where God the Holy Spirit is most active as Jesus calms the winds of rebellion which have so roiled up the waters in the reflecting pool of our lives. With the Holy Spirit we now, like never before, have the perfect equipment to reflect "the Image of God."

The Unity of the Trinity

Consider the awesome coordination between your Body and Soul. Your mind gets an idea to reach for a pencil: we do not understand just how, but the message goes from the Soul (mind) to the Body, and the hand reaches over to pick up the pencil! The coordination is *seamless*: two very different parts, Soul and Body, each having its unique area of ability, work together without any awareness as to where the one leaves off and the other begins.

Prick a finger with a pin and the Soul feels the pain. Should the Body be faint from hunger, the great words of wisdom which the Soul is formulating may not make much sense. Even in the Spirit's activity – such as praying – generally the mind and the Body are involved. How, we do not know, yet all three parts work simply as a seamless unity. On the other hand, something like epilepsy appears to identify when this seamlessness is challenged.

So, in this way, in a mirror made of frail human material is displayed the *Image* of the Great Creator of the universe in the full wonder of His three Persons within a seamless unity. But as mentioned earlier, this mirror Image can demonstrate only certain characteristics and in a limited way, as a

10

"surface" resemblance, compared to the enormous scope of characteristics which the Divine Trinity has. We are merely three parts in one self; He is three separate Persons in one seamless God. Although the human "Image of God" expresses a marvelous reality about our Creator, it falls short in revealing the fullness of what the Divine Trinity is like.

Soul – Life – Blood

> But flesh in its Soul/Life – its Blood – you shall not eat. … Whoever sheds man's Blood, by man his Blood shall be shed; for in the Image of God He made man.
>
> Genesis 9:4,6

Particularly here, in Leviticus 17:11,14 and in Deuteronomy 12:23, the word for "Soul" – translated as "Life" – is equated with "Blood." This combination of concepts surrounding "Blood" is especially important in regard to a central theme of the Bible, Covenant. When Covenant is cut between individuals, each opens a wound and mingles their Bloods, with the understanding that now as their Bloods are one, so also their Lives, so also their Souls – *they* are now one (such as Jonathan and David's Covenant in I Samuel 18:1-3).

This has profound impact and implication in relation to Jehovah's intent and heart's-desire in His Covenants with humans.[1] But the precursor and foundation to Covenant is what God declares in Genesis 1:26 (also 5:1):

Then God said, "Let us make man in Our Image, after Our *Likeness*"

The Hebrew word for "Likeness" [*damah*] is derived from the word for "Blood" [Hebrew *dam*] – its meaning would be "Blood-Likeness," or as defined above, "Life-Likeness," or "Soul-Likeness." In fact, man's whole origin is immersed with the concept of Blood: "Blood" is the source for the Hebrew words for "man" or "humanity" [*Adam*] and the "ground" [*adamah*] from which he is created [Genesis 2·7] Standing inside this Covenant relationship, Adam and Eve have access to all the Life of God, and His "Soul" flows through them.

On our side of the Fall into Sin, we probably cannot fully comprehend what all this exactly means, but it does impress us with the extraordinary closeness to Himself that Jehovah has intended humanity to have. It also reveals just what the loss means when we in rebellion step outside of this extraordinary relationship. No wonder God would describe it as *death*.

It also helps us understand more about "the New Covenant," which is not a doctrine, but rather *the Person* of Jesus. In Him God and Man are joined by the same Blood: cut Jesus and Man bleeds, but so does God! Kill Jesus and Man dies, but so does God! In order to recover the "Blood" relationship with Jehovah that Adam and Eve had enjoyed at the beginning, we must be in Jesus, in His LifeBlood – or as St Paul puts it, "in Christ."

The Badge of Authority

When Henry M. Stanley searched Africa for Dr. Livingstone, he cut Covenants with various tribes. In one such Covenant, a powerful chief gave him a scepter wrapped with brass bands. This badge of authority guaranteed that throughout that area of Africa, Stanley would be treated with honor and respect – the might of the chief was behind him.[2]

So also humankind, created in "the Image of God," with the "Blood (Soul/Life)-Likeness" of God and bearing "the Breath of God," carries Jehovah's "Badge of Authority"; the "Likeness" of the very Soul of God. This is his equipment to fulfill his task before all Creation, which in response gives him the honor and respect appropriate for the Creator's representative.

The Agent

Now carrying his "Badge of Authority" ("the Image of God") before all Creation, and given his commission, Adam is placed into the Garden of Eden "to tend (work or serve) it and keep (preserve or guard) it" [Genesis 2:15]. He represents not himself, but the visible exercise of God's authority and care over Creation. So significant is his place in managing the physical Creation, this "cosmos," that this responsibility will be done by no other creature. If man does not take on his charge, then Creation will and does suffer.

Jehovah God ratifies both Adam's authority and position by bringing the animals to him "to see what he would call them, and whatever Adam called each 'living creature,' that was its name" [v 19].

The Glory

St Paul ties the Image to the picture of God's Glory:

> But we all, with unveiled face, beholding the Glory of the Lord as in a mirror, are being transformed into the same Image from Glory to Glory, exactly as from the Lord the Spirit.   II Corinthians 3:18

In Exodus 33:18-19, Moses asks to see Jehovah's Glory and the Lord's immediate response is interesting: there is no emphasis on His power, His majesty, His government, not even on the honor and praise due Him. No, what Moses shall see is His goodness, Covenant relationship, grace, and mercy. Then in 34:6-8, Steadfast Love (HESED)[3], faithfulness, forgiveness and justice are added. Apparently these are the characteristics which God especially regards as His Glory. So when man, as the mirror of "the Image of God," reveals the characteristics that should make the Creator recognizable to Creation, of how little importance are might and control compared to these qualities (which we shall view in more detail later). This seems to be in keeping with Jesus' teaching:

> Having called them to Him, Jesus said, "You know that the rulers of the nations exercise lordship over them, and their great ones exercise authority over them. It shall not be so among you; but whoever would become great among you must be your servant, and whoever would be first among you must be your slave; even as the Son of Man came not to be served but to serve, and to give His life as a Ransom for many."
>
> Matthew 20:25-28

The Exclusive Clique

> I am Jehovah, that is My Name; My Glory I give to no other, nor My praise to carved images.
>
> Isaiah 42:8

> ... lest you act corruptly and make for yourselves a carved image in the form of any figure, in the likeness of male or female, in the likeness of any beast that is on the earth, the likeness of any winged bird that flies in the sky, in the likeness of anything that creeps on the ground, in the likeness of any fish that is in the water under the earth.
>
> Deuteronomy 4:16-18

God's design is that He has only one Image on this earth: humankind. Yet humanity are not an end to itself (an idol of itself), which is what Satan suggests to Adam and Eve. Rather as a mirror filled with its Subject, it is to be a dynamic reflection of God, always the pointer to the Original. Anything less distorts the picture of God, which the Creator will not tolerate.

3. Male and Female He Created Them

Emphasis on the Genders

> So God created the man in His Image, in the Image of God created He him; *male and female created He them.*   Genesis 1:27

This passage is echoed in chapter 5: "… In the day that God created man, He made him in the Blood[/Soul/Life]-Likeness of God. *He created them male and female …*" [vv 1-2]. It is puzzling. So what that humankind is created as "male and female" – are not all higher animals "male and female"? Why should there be such an emphasis for *only* the human?

The Basis in the Image

"The Image of God" and the "Blood-likeness of God" are interlocked with "male and female" – could this be a clue? The "Image" and "Likeness" accents the mystery of Jehovah's choice: more than just a reflection of Him, we humans are made to be *essential* as He reveals Himself to the universe. This responsibility is not a part-time role for us, as if it were some sort of recreational option; rather it describes our basic identity, *a reason why we exist at all.* We are so designed that when all Creation looks at us at any time and at any place, it should catch the picture of God.

Consider, for example, the aid given the man left for dead in the parable of the Good Samaritan, or feeding those in a famine, or sharing the Gospel. Similar to when a parent refuses to do a child's duties or chores for him, so also the angels will not do these things for us, nor will God step in to do them Himself. Jehovah is that committed in making us true partners with

Himself, seeking that we be "faithful over a few things" so that He might make us "ruler over many things" [Matthew 25:21].

When, in Genesis 2, the man and the woman are separately created with deliberate emphasis surrounding each act of creation, there is the implication that more is at work here than that the two are merely counterparts for procreation. There are aspects involved for which the umbrella terms of "human" and "humankind" are just not adequate – there is something so unique about the male and the female individually that the listener/reader must be reminded about *both*.

The Binocular of the Genders

Each gender is equipped with certain traits and characteristics, which we refer to as "masculine" and "feminine." Just where do these traits come from in the first place? Are they merely the product of human contrivance, or do they run deeper than that? Are they merely options from which to pick and choose what appeals to us and to discard what gets in our way, or are there more profound meanings to them? Are they some sort of evolutionary accretion that we should "throw off" now that we have "progressed further"?

Our existence is defined by the "Image" and "Likeness" of God – that is the given reason why we have been created. Therefore these masculine and feminine traits do not spring from within us – they are not "our property" – *He* is the Source of all the traits always. What is "masculine" or "feminine" is not culturally determined "a la mode," nor is one to be declared as "superior" or "inferior." Instead, these traits are *Jehovah's chosen way* through which *He* will demonstrate *Himself* in each of us, in and because of each gender.

Each of our two eyes sees basically the same thing, but there is enough variation in perspective that together the eyes provide an extraordinary enhancement. A whole additional dimension comes into reality; now we are able to see in *three* dimensions with a fullness which modern movies are just attempting to capture. Likewise the human genders reflect the same God: on the one hand, the male and the female with their own distinctive traits exhibit to Creation their unique perspective on essential hallmarks of the Creator; but then *together* they reveal a new depth or fullness to *His* "Image."

Actually the principle of two viewpoints is common in the Scriptures, even to where the Bible itself is set up as a binocular view of God – the Old and the New Testaments. Both declare the same God, and basically the same things about Him, yet there are differences to each perspective, so that together there is a far more complete "Image" of Jehovah than would be available separately.

The Different "Oculars"

There are differences between these two human creatures. In the organization of the male brain, the hemispheres are more independent and separated from each other. A baby boy responds more to geometric shapes and as he grows, tends to be more task- and performance-oriented. He tends toward analytic thinking: examining, lining up the pieces, and drawing his conclusions.

The female brain hemispheres have more interconnection. Even as a baby girl, she responds more to faces, touch, pain; and tends to be more relationship-oriented. She tends toward synthetic thinking, grasping the situation as a mosaic whole – probably the source of the celebrated "woman's intuition."

That said, obviously the different tendencies and traits are not *exclusive* to either sex, and can be present to a greater or a lesser degree in everyone. However, if there is to be a binocular effect, then there indeed still must be enough difference – if both eyes were to see identically then there would be no benefit to having two. But the deliberate design, as expressed in the organic difference even of the brain, is that the two genders should have enough dissimilarity so as to bring out the fullness of Jehovah's Image.

The problem is that we really do not know what to do about gender uniqueness. So often we disregard or ignore it, especially as being "not politically correct." Yet at the same time, when it can be "used" to support a sort of arrogance over the other gender, it will be paraded with condescension. Very rarely does one come across any real thankfulness (not a veiled put-down) for the God-given differences, where both sets of abilities are considered necessary in showing the attributes essential for a balanced "three-dimensional" view of our Creator.

Jehovah in "3-D"

The traits of the genders are powerful: they determine who we see ourselves to be, what we are about, even our value and worth. When attempts are made to distinguish the differences without reference to the stated task of humanity, that is, "the Image of God," and are therefore disconnected from Jehovah, these things will then often bring confusion and struggle, hostility and envy, superiority conflict and rejection. The male and the female must start from the position that each step they take, each expression of their gender, *must* reveal *God* according to His design, through the uniqueness of the traits bestowed upon them, to those around them. Only then will they realize that in the Holy Spirit's power they are prophets: they declare the mind, heart and will of the Creator to His Creation.

This combined approach between the genders gives what would otherwise seem like fanciful or vague abstract ideas an explicit, touchable, meaningful and real-world expression. So, borrowing from I John 1:1-2, "God Loves you," "God cares about you," "God will uphold you," "God forgives you," and any other such statements now can be actually "heard ... seen with our eyes ... looked upon ... handled ... manifested ... witnessed," in the full dimensions of both masculine and feminine expression. This passage can be applied to these statements because, by Baptism, Male and Female are made the Body of Christ, and therefore comes a real connection to His presence and to His "Image of God" in this world.

Whether it be in the areas of spirituality, morality, compassion, discipline, or whatever it may be, as these humans make their home, run their family, bring up their children, go about their daily occupations and vocations, and generally manage Creation, as Jehovah expresses His traits through them, they together are the "3-D" Image of Him. And their children, as well as others, catch a glimpse of the actual God Who stands behind what they are and what they do.

Distortion in the Mirror

The Creator's design has been terribly distorted by sin. Satan's sales line haunts us even today. Rather than a reflection which points to Him, we want to "become just like God" [Genesis 3:5], able to do all things, to be all things, to be basically self-sufficient (especially independent from God), to be complete in and of ourselves. We want to point to ourselves.

We think that the issue deals with what is best for our career, what can we accumulate, or any other thing we think governs our lives. Rather the true question is whether we are fulfilling the purpose of our creation, that of being "the Image of God," because if not, then there is no way in which we can find any sort of real and continuing satisfaction in our existence. This is part of Jesus' call to "seek first the Kingdom of God and His righteousness, and all these things shall be added to you" [Matthew 6:33].

But the binocular view adds an even greater context: there is no way we can fulfill that purpose in our creation without recognizing the partnership we must have with the opposite gender. We just cannot do this adequately alone – in fact, that is precisely what the Creator Himself said!

Yet we are reluctant to need each other, except for our own ends. We rebel against the extraordinary honor and responsibility which Jehovah has placed upon the two genders together. We act as if the masculine or the feminine traits are merely expressions of our own selves, reflecting only our fleeting ideals; we may despise our own or the other gender's traits; we may ignore the traits as if they have no real significance; we may treat them as merely cultural burdens imposed by generations of misguided people or even repressed fools. Or if the difference is within the biological, then we seek to make them technologically immaterial.

Turning away from the Creator and refusing His will ... if only we can manipulate the genes just right, or the psychology, or the environment ... if only we ... We want to tweak ourselves into whatever is the current idea of perfection, not so unlike the Nazi attempt to breed the "super race." Rick Evans' "In the Year 2525 (Exordium and Terminus)" gives us pause to consider:

> In the year 3535
> Ain't gonna need to tell the truth, tell no lie
> Everything you think, do and say
> Is in the pill you took today.[4]

The overriding theme, of a world doomed by its passive acquiescence to and overdependence on its own overdone technologies, struck a resonant chord in millions of people around the world in the late 1960s.[5]

We want the instant fast-fix which will automate our lives based upon a "cookie-cutter" existence. We turn from the unique, hand-crafted vision of Adam's, and then of Eve's, Creation, with the specialness of each. To realize each's uniqueness includes the challenge and hard work to truly get to know the human in front of us who is definitely not some extension of ourselves, nor of our perceptions, nor of our abilities, nor of our desires, but rather is the product of God's deliberate and different design. How often we demand that the opposite gender be a duplicate of ourselves: they must see things as we do, think as we do, reason as we do, have the same values and priorities as we do. They were never meant to, yet how fast we can turn to rejection, anger, ridicule, and even violence to force them into our own image.

We toy, for example, with the concept of "unisex," which attempts to have no gender identity at all, homogenizing everyone into a featureless monotony. However, this "ideal" is constantly frustrated because a simple walk down a busy street reveals that gender is obviously ingrained into our genetic make-up, and as one observes people's perspectives and interests (for example, "girl" and "guy" movies), gender apparently is ingrained into the Soul and Spirit as well. Or we look to the artificial models of magazine and film screen and judge each other based on a fantasy that has little to do with the Creator's expression of *His* complexity in us. Homosexual marriage, especially with its attempt to have children by adoption or artificial insemination, is the attempt to dispense with the need of an opposite gender, and reflects the rebellion against Jehovah's spiritual intent for "the male" and "the female" representation of His nature.

"I Do Not Need You"

When God says "It is not good that the man should be alone" [Genesis 2:18], it stands in contrast to our modern society, where we struggle with whether we really want to need anyone else. We "cocoon" – build into our houses everything we need in order to avoid an unpredictable world, much less to physically interact with anyone else. Our entertainment centers surround us so as to control our increasingly vicarious life; our internet convinces us of our "connection to the world," and yet we do not know our neighbor next door; rarely do we really get beyond our "Facebook" friends' façades; and should we get a text message on the iPhone, we de-humanize the person we are with, shutting down to him/her, and making the text message and its reply the most important focus of the moment.

Yet there is a deep frustration: the Creator's simple statement reflects our genetic foundation . We would like to say, "I do not need ...," but it just exaggerates the heartfelt loneliness. Since there is no true community, no actual involvement, no effective participation – no real enthusiasm for sharing life – the emptiness simply sops up our life like a sponge. But when someone actually touches our hand, our shoulder, our face, we are affirmed as important, that we are alive, that we are *real*. We realize that Jehovah is right after all: it is not good to be alone, we do need each other.

But others are not physically, mentally, psychologically, or spiritually identical to us, not even in facial and body characteristics. Too often, farthest from our minds is how Jehovah is expressing Himself through the people we meet and deal with each day – a truly daunting task for most of us to handle, especially where one has to look hard to discover Him in some people.

A "Significant" Other

Alright then, how about the one-to-one of a spouse? As the Lord brings Eve to Adam, the message to both is that *here* is what each needs to fill that emptiness, a void which is not merely human loneliness but also the emptiness of not having God's "Image" "visible" before them. Without this reflection there will be a restless dissatisfaction which "church" still may not answer. It is essential that "the Image" and "the Soul-likeness" is not just what we reflect, but what must be reflected to us; we need to *see* Him especially through this closest human in our lives, for without this, there will always be a certain emptiness.

Should we not see Him in our spouse, then is this a good reason to dispense with the mate? Or rather is it that one's "ocular" of our "binocular" needs to be adjusted? Have we fallen victim to the distortions in *our* own mirror, as just described in the last section, through which we fail to see the distinctive way in which God chooses to reveal Himself in this most significant human in our lives? God's message to both Adam and Eve is that this spouse is exactly what the other needs, even when one thinks that the other is not what he/she *wants* at this moment.

The challenge then is to come to terms not only with the words, "I love you," but especially with the words, "I need you." It means that the couple does not fight about the differences between "male and female," nor despises them, but cherishes them and discovers how together they become more sensitive to their Lord's revelation of Himself to and through them.

It is no secret, though, that even when working together, because of sin, "male and female" will fall far short of being that "Image of God" which had been the design from the beginning. An image is reflected only insofar as the reflecting material is able, and when that material has been contaminated and twisted – consider the "fun house" distorted mirrors –

not only does the reflection lose clarity, it can also lose the subject that it is to reflect. Even this "Image" needs a Savior.

The Genders Par Excellence

There is One Who is the perfect reflection – Image – of God [II Corinthians 4:4; Colossians 1:15]. More than that, He actually is Jehovah Himself come in the flesh, Jesus [John 1:1]. However, St Paul in Ephesians 5:31-32 makes a most curious statement: after quoting the marriage verse from Genesis 2 ("A man leaves father and mother ..."), he declares that this statement applies specifically to Jesus, but not to Him alone – the counterpart is the Bride which is the Church [v 32; also see vv 21-30]. On one hand it is indeed a beautiful picture of love, commitment and the rest of those elements that make up this relationship.

But what particularly raises an eyebrow is to think of this relationship in terms of the "binocular" view of God in the genders, which is so powerfully represented within marriage. Most obviously, Jesus should be all-sufficient by Himself as the complete "Image of God." A "second gender," His Bride, should be most unnecessary. However, it is curious as we look at the Ephesians passage and find that Paul does not compare the "marriage" of Jesus and His Bride to an earthly husband and wife, but rather the human relationship takes its cue from the heavenly Couple – so the "binocular" view of God between spouses about which we have been discussing should actually *start* with the eternal Bridegroom and Bride. Paul seems to even indicate that it is *Jesus* about Whom the Father would say, "It is not good that the Man should be alone; I will make Him a helper fitting for Him" [Genesis 2:18]. It appears, then, that the Bride of Christ is *required* if we are to have a true 3-D view of God!

This returns us to the bewilderment of why Jehovah chooses to make us indispensable, yet Paul reminds us that when God creates the woman she is but a reflection of Jesus' Bride. What we see, then, in her role is simply making visible what the Church is about – what *we* are about.

"The Image" Who Saves

As Ephesians 5 identifies, even from the very beginning of humanity, there is a specific model for the man and the woman to follow, despite how it has been millennia between the pronouncement in Genesis and its fulfillment in Jesus and His Church. Yet this statement can be misleading: what Jesus and His Bride do is not for the sake of providing a model, but rather Jesus is being the Husband, the Masculine side, and in so doing, He is *saving* men and *saving* women. It is not for the sake of a show, nor for some sort of an object lesson. He genuinely has sacrificed Himself so that His Bride actually lives.

Jesus has willingly given up His own "comfort and security" for His Bride – He has left His Father and turned away from the throne of heaven. He has no basis for conceit, "no form or comeliness that we should look at Him, and no beauty that we should desire Him" [Isaiah 53:2:]; He washes feet; He suffers unjustly; He is abandoned by His closest friends; He is betrayed by one in His inner circle; He is forsaken even by His Father; He experiences total loneliness; He is "despised and rejected … One from Whom people hid their faces" [Isaiah 53:3]; He is misunderstood; and the list goes much longer.

All this as this "Husband" gives Himself up, sacrifices Himself for His Bride, both in the big and in the little things, in their task to reflect "the Image" in this world. His Blood/Life/Soul is poured out and *into* this relationship. This is not merely a "model" of what the masculine may involve, beyond the authority and control which often is emphasized, rather this is the actual experience of the One Whom men are to follow.

As well, His Bride, as she submits – is totally committed – to her Beloved, also experiences hardship, suffering, bondage, martyrdom for the sake of her love. *Her* Blood/Life/Soul also is poured out and *into* this relationship in response to what He has done. Paul does not refer the human women to the Bride of Christ in a trivial or condescending way. As a member of that Bride, he lists for the Corinthians [II, 11:23-29] some of the demands that this relationship to the Bride's Husband has required.

Yet it is also in this very letter that he declares:

> But we all, with unveiled face, beholding the Glory of the Lord as in a mirror, are being transformed into the same Image from Glory to Glory, exactly as from the Lord the Spirit. II Corinthians 3:18

Jesus has taken us by the hand and through His Spirit He leads us into a Life which we would never have otherwise known. This bond between Jesus and His Bride is very much real-life, demanding but also creative, bringing each of us to actually become the reflections of this Woman with this Man in this eternal relationship.

As a side note, some religions declare that when Eve takes of the fruit of the forbidden tree, Adam is faced with a dilemma: either to not sin and therefore be unable to fulfill the command to multiply and fill the earth, or to sin so that he and his wife can obey that command. So in great nobility and "self-sacrifice" he also sins. How really big-hearted of him.

But as indicated above, if he is to reflect Jesus, Adam, still perfect and sinless, would have chosen to *die* in order to trade his life for Eve's, to *save* his wife. After all, this is what Jesus has done because of *His great Love for His Bride, the Church, the People of His rescuing.* And just as, when called upon to sacrifice Isaac [Genesis 22:1-19], Abraham expected a resurrection if

26

necessary [Hebrews 11:17-19], so also Adam would have to depend on Jehovah's solution, even a resurrection if necessary in order to get everything back on its proper track. No, this Adam instead refused to take ownership of the position given to him by his Creator, and therefore comes the rest of the Bible.

This contrast between "the two Adams" [I Corinthians 15:45] is useful in our discussion: only as we realize how essential it is that we reflect this eternal couple of Jesus with His Bride will we then discover how we reveal "the Image of God" in a binocular perspective that brings the depth of God to light:

> that, according to the riches of His Glory, He would make you become strong with power through His Spirit in the inner man, that Christ may dwell through faith in your hearts; that you, being rooted and founded in Love, may a full capacity to comprehend with all the saints what is the width, length, depth and height, and to know with transcending knowledge the Love of Christ; that you may be filled with all the fullness of God.   Ephesians 3:16-19

4. The Man: Subdue and Have Dominion

The Commission

Now that humanity is so equipped, just what is their task?

> God said, "Let Us make man in Our Image, according to Our Likeness: and let them rule over the fish of the sea, over the birds of the heavens, over the cattle and over all the earth, and over all the creeping things which creep upon the earth" So God created the man in His Image, in the Image of God created He him; male and female created He them. God blessed them, and God said to them, "Be fruitful and multiply, and fill the earth and subdue it; and rule over the fish of the sea, over the birds of the heavens and over all creeping beasts upon the earth."
>
> Genesis 1:26-28

Bearing the sign of God's "Image" and "Soul-Likeness," humankind is authorized to carry out God's management of Creation, and, possessing this extraordinary resource, they are also accountable to God. They have the charge to "subdue" and "have dominion" – they are to bring Creation not merely under their rule, as if for their own pleasure, but ultimately under the rule of *their* Lord. It is the task that is happening right now in regard to Jesus (our "Head" – see chapter 10), Whom

> ... the Father of Glory ... raised ... from the dead and having seated Him at His right hand in the heavenly places, far above every principality and authority and power and dominion and every name named, not only in this age, but also in the coming one; and all things He put under His feet, and gave Him to be head over all things *for the Church*, which is His Body, the fullness of Him Who fill all in all.
>
> Ephesians 1:17, 20-23

Although the Creator has entrusted this responsibility to "them" and therefore this is a joint task, still the man is given the initial charge and therefore has a significant role. Before Eve is created, Adam is placed into the Garden to begin this commission [Genesis 2:15]; he names (therefore has power over) the animals brought to him [vv 19-20], and he even gives the woman *her* permanent identification, "Eve," "Mother of all Living" [3:20] (her name for him we will never know, which is perhaps just as well). She is called "the Helper" by God, although, as we will see later, this word must be used carefully. Jehovah turns not to the woman, but rather first to the man to "own up" after the first sin. As the opening chapters of the Bible play out, although both share in the commission, the man's role has a crucial impact.

Of Chairs and Fathers

As "the Image of God," it is inevitable that the man's role should reflect the Creator as "Father." However, to understand what this and other key words mean in this study, we need to examine how often such meanings are connected to experience.

For example, when we were young, we learned what a "chair" was because that was the name of the thing people sat on. Over time, we learned that other objects which did not look quite the same were also "chairs." Some were basically wooden frames, others were fluffed and stuffed; some took up very little space, others occupied a great deal of room; some were rigid, others leaned so far backwards and gave you a footrest; some gently rocked, others vibrated – yet they were all "chairs."

We moved from the *object* of a "chair" to the *essence* or *essential characteristics* of a "chair" – we began to recognize chair-like things. Perhaps the shape of tree roots suggests a chair to us. Modern materials are used to make really odd looking chairs – yet chairs nonetheless. When we shop for furniture, we look for what will be the "perfect" chair for our needs.

30

From the *essence* we moved on to the *symbolic* character of a "chair." The word speaks of authority, for instance, as the one who runs the meeting is the "chair," or a learned professor holds the "chair" of a particular subject at a university.

This progression of understanding happens probably with every noun that we know, and especially has happened with the word "Father." For most of us, we learned about that word based on a particular man when we were young. Over time, we observed other fathers. Some were basically "wooden frames," others were "fluffed and stuffed"; some took up very little space, others occupied a great deal of room; some were rigid, others leaned so far backwards and gave you a footrest; some gently rocked, others vibrated – yet they were all "fathers."

Over the years, we went on to formulate an idea of what the essential characteristics of a father should be. Sometimes we realized that there was a gap between what we originally experienced as a "father" and what we now desire that a "father" should be, what an *ideal* father would be. Perhaps that ideal is very close to what we had experienced, although with a few modifications, of course. But sometimes that ideal is in stark contrast to our experiences: the father we wished we had; the father we wished we could get close to, and could get close to us; the father we would want to be when *we* become fathers ourselves.

Looking for "the Image of God"

This has an important link in regard to "the Image of God," since it is not long before the symbolic concept of "father" extends to our vision of what the Creator – Who has chosen to call Himself "Father" – is all about. It is not in a worship service or a Bible study where a child first forms "the Image" of what will be God's attitudes, His trustworthiness, His use of power and so much more. As he totally depends on the ones who have ultimate control of his existence, so often it is in the home where he will shape his concepts of love and being loved, of his value and worth, and even of the impression of whether this world is a good place to be Obviously he is not thinking in those terms, but he is learning through how he experiences the representatives of the Lord.

Such experiences often dictate whether Jehovah is seen as a frightening Object or One of love and care. This is an awesome and humbling responsibility, and sadly one where many fathers do not realize – or do not want to know – just how significant they are in their child's view of the Lord. It is a responsibility that demands extreme care because of the lifetime of effect that it has, and sometimes the result must be overcome with great difficulty in order for the child to have a proper view of God.

The balance in this is that meanwhile "our Father" does not stop fulfilling this role *for us*. As fathers discover the depths of *the Lord*'s true fatherhood to them, then they are enabled for themselves to "be imitators of God as dear children" [Ephesians 5:1]. And the idea of "Fatherhood," in reflecting "the Original," includes not just one's own immediate family. It extends outward to encompass Creation, since that is included in the commission of being "the Image of God," so that even those without children, even without families, are not excluded from this important appointment.

This does not underplay the role of the mother (as we will see), but simply emphasizes how the father cannot be derelict in his commission, and that he cannot merely delegate this responsibility to anyone else. His role is just too key to be treated with indifference.

The Language of "Subdue"

One of the first tasks that the human, significantly the man, is given is "to subdue" Creation. It is useful to note that although "child" is the reference point in the above discussion, "Creation" could be substituted without doing much violence to the thought. Here again, the words need to be examined if the man – and the woman – are to correctly understand how "subdue" fits into "the Image of God" as revealed through them. *The Theological Wordbook of the Old Testament* [*TWOT*] says of the Hebrew word for "subdue":

> Despite recent interpretations of Gen 1:28 which have tried to make 'subdue' mean a responsibility for building up, it is obvious from an overall study of the word's usage that this is not so. *kabash* assumes that the party being subdued is hostile to the subduer, necessitating some sort of coercion if the subduing is to take place. Thus the word connotes 'rape' in Est 7:8, or the conquest of the Canaanites in Num 32:22,29; Josh 18:1; I Chr 22:18. In II Chr 28:10; Neh 5:5; Jer 34:11,16 it refers to forced servitude.
>
> Therefore 'subdue' in Gen 1:28 implies that creation will not do man's bidding gladly or easily and that man must now bring creation into submission by main strength. It is not to rule man. However, there is a twistedness in humanity which causes us to perform such a task with fierce and destructive delight. Try as we might, we cannot subdue this. But it can be subdued and this is the promise of Mic 7:10, 'He will subdue our iniquities.'

When the above writer identifies that what is being subdued (Creation) is *hostile* to the subduer (Adam), this is awkward. The idea of hostility is understandable if the setting is *after* the first sin, when God declares: "Cursed is the ground because of you; in toil you shall eat of it all the days of your life; thorns and thistles it shall bring forth for you ..." [Genesis 3:17-18]. Creation now will rebel against the rebel and the idea of hostility is now indeed in line with the other passages noted in the *TWOT* quote.

But when God is first giving the humans their charge, sin has not yet entered into "the very good" Creation [1:31]. Enmity, quarrel, defiance – all those things are really quite out of place at this point. Could there be a sense to "subdue" different here in the *before* of sin, since the conditions are still a perfect and "very good" Creation in contrast to the other twelve places in the Bible which describe this *after* the Fall?

The limitations of human languages raise their heads here: the meaning of words depends heavily upon our experience. For example, "tree" has its meaning because we have experienced one; so also for "chair." A profound example is to explain color to a person born blind. The difficulty in explaining intangible things such as "love," "grace," and "faith" is that somehow they have to hook into a common experience if they are to go beyond merely nice sounding, but ultimately meaningless words – *as well as* to avoid the danger of bland and puny definitions. Imagine the difficulty of Ezekiel, John and others in using human-experience words to describe the extremely out-of-human-experience visions of heaven – and of our subsequent confusion as we try to figure out from our experience what is being described in these visions.

Other words can also be very tricky. Hebrews 5:8 says, "though [Jesus] was a Son, yet He learned obedience by the things which He suffered." Does that mean that a) He was originally disobedient, or b) He was ignorant of obedience, or c) one would never know just how obedient He was until He was pushed to his very limits in which the degree of His obedience was now plainly seen? The last option is the meaning in this passage – which identifies how close attention must be paid to the context of the words in order to understand their meanings, particularly in the Bible.

The problem with "subdue" is that it is defined from a set of our experiences which have occurred only after sin and rebellion have entered and corrupted Creation. But what of the state of things before such resistance existed?

Consider the situation: Creation is wild, not hostile. It is not tame, not because it refuses to be, but rather because it never has been – in fact, there is no "has been." According to the King James translation of Genesis 1:15, Adam is placed into the Garden of Eden "to dress it and to keep it"; the Revised Standard Version puts it "to till it and keep it." Never has this happened to Creation – not that it is unwilling to be conformed to the will of man, it just is unfamiliar territory. Never was the ground broken in order to grow only a certain seed, never were the fruit trees pruned in order to direct their energies into larger fruit, never were crops rotated in order to allow the land to rest and recuperate properly, never were the grape vines fixed to a lattice so as to make best use of the sun, never was the donkey used to transport items, never was the horse ridden, never was a cow milked for man's enjoyment – and the list goes on and on.

"Subdue" would be quite a proper word here, in order to make Creation conform to man's will, as well as to discover and to coordinate with its own needs – which does not require the hostile environment which the *TWOT* quote implies. Creation would go through a learning curve as it comes to understand what is expected of it. Imagine the horse the first time Adam sat on it (assuming he did). The animal would not be hostile nor rejecting Adam, but would be bewildered and surprised, wondering what this was all about. He would have to learn to be controlled, perhaps by some sort of reining or leg control. But also Adam would have to learn how to work with this animal's abilities, what could be done and how best to do it as he teaches the horse to obey his commands.

On this order, one wonders if "horse whispering," which is a method of gently forming a bond with a horse, is perhaps a window on the relationship which Adam once enjoyed with Creation.

Mirror, Curb, and Guide

> But this is the Covenant that I will cut with the house of Israel after those days, says Jehovah: I will put My Law (*torah*) in their inward parts, and write it on their hearts; I will be their God, and they shall be My People. Jeremiah 31:33

As Adam literally "starts from scratch," he will have to lay down some basic operating conventions, so that when he presses his left leg into the horse's side, the horse should go left (or right); or so that a potato crop cannot be planted in the same area for two years in a row, or whatever the rule may be.

In Christian theology, such "oughts," "shoulds," and "musts" are called "the Law," even though these rules may not have a harsh or condemnatory character to them. Adam and Eve themselves are subject to one such command in regard to the Tree of Knowledge.

"The Law" is said to have three roles: mirror, curb, and guide. The "mirror" shows us what we are like, which means that after the Fall into Sin, it reveals our sinfulness. But the Fall has not yet happened – in fact, Adam and Eve are not even conscious of themselves until after they eat of the forbidden fruit, so that this role of the "Law" is immaterial at this time. Actually, *they* are the mirror that reflects God and His will.

The "Curb" means that the "Law," after the Fall, can restrain us from doing wrong. But Jeremiah [31:33] prophesies that after the New Covenant comes, the "Law" will already be in the heart rather than imposed from the outside. Also, again, we are here looking at *before* the Fall. If Adam "lays down the Law" to Creation, is there a place within "subdue" where "curb" would fit, yet not within a hostile environment? It is hard to know what a perfect animal in a perfect world would do, but suppose the cow needs to learn that the vegetable and flower gardens are not for her – is lack of comprehension a sign of hostility? Is it a sign of antagonism if she needs a repeated lesson to finally realize this "rule" about gardens, even though every place else to which she goes is not restricted? Can there be a "wrong" which is not sin, where not all "wrong" is in rebellion? (The irony of the cow's predicament is how it is quite similar to the prohibition placed on Adam and Eve not to eat of *the Tree of Knowledge* – however, unlike the cow, *they* understood from the beginning what is forbidden, so that their rebellion has no excuse.)

As a "Guide," the rules or Law would indicate what is to be done and how it will get done. For the ox to be "subdued" to the will of Adam as it learns how to pull a plow, it must respond to commands which must be learned as to when to stop or to go or to turn – it is compelled to conform, even though there is no deliberate resistance on its part. In fact, one would expect that it would be very compliant.

In addition, in the Old Testament, the word which is translated as "Law" is *torah*, which has a much broader understanding:

> The word tôrâ means basically 'teaching' whether it is the wise man instructing his son or God instructing Israel. The wise give insight into all aspects of life so that the young may know how to conduct themselves and to live a long blessed life. {Pr 3:1f} So too God, motivated by love, reveals to man basic insight into how to live with each other and how to approach God....
>
> In addition, the book of Deut itself shows that the law has a broad meaning to encompass history, regulations and their interpretation, and exhortations. It is not merely the listing of casuistic statements as is the case in Hammurabi's code. Later the word was extended to include the first five books of the Bible in all their variety.   *TWOT*[7]

As indicated, the *torah* actually contains a wealth of material greater than what one might crassly put as "the rules and regulations"; and especially in its teaching capacity, it would support very well the proposed pre-sin understanding of "subdue."

After the Flood

When the world is "born anew" after Noah's flood, there is a radical difference in the commission given to Noah and his family:

> God blessed Noah and his sons, and said to them: "Be fruitful and multiply, and fill the earth. The fear and the dread of you shall be on every beast of the earth, on every bird of heaven, on all that moves on the earth, and on all the fish of the sea. Into your hand they are given. Every moving thing which lives shall be food for you. Even as the green plants, I have given you all things." Genesis 9:1-3

Rather than "There is no fear in the Love; but the perfect Love casts out the fear, because the fear has torment" [I John 4:18], which would describe the conditions of the original Creation, "fear" and "dread" are here introduced and the animals now even become food themselves. These are concepts of a *new* "subdue" which were never in the original context, and, most interestingly, *that* word is not used in this parallel command, in fact, it is not used until Numbers 32, where the Promised Land will be "subdued."[8] Does its omission with Noah accent the deliberate difference in this setting from the original environment of what God has entrusted to humanity?

And different it is. Who knows what the humans did before the flood, but by the time our modern world has set foot on this earth, there was and is gross exploitation of resources and disregard for this precious charge which God has given us. The "However, there is a twistedness in humanity which causes us to perform such a task with fierce and destructive delight" of the *TWOT* quote in the opening pages of this chapter is *now* the background for man's activity. The quote seems also to infer that humankind cannot even "subdue" his own nature, much less that of his now rebellious and hostile charge.

Dominion

"Dominion" would be the follow-up of "subdue": "subdue" establishes the leadership, and "dominion" is the everyday administration of that rule. According to "the Image" and "Soul-Likeness" of God, when Creation looks at Adam, it should see the reflection of its Creator in all His Glory – the Glory as previously identified[9]: His goodness, Covenant relationship, grace, mercy, Steadfast Love, faithfulness, forgiveness and justice. So not only in the "subduing," but also in the "dominion" must these pivotal attributes clearly reign supreme. Humankind is God's agent, His ambassador, "the courier" between Creator and Creation, the high priest or pastor of the "cosmos", bringing to the Lord its needs, praise and worship (as suggested in the call to all nature to worship [Psalm 148; Isaiah 44:23; 49:13; 55:12-13]).

Is such a romantic idealization of *Creation*'s ability to praise Jehovah a mere fantasy, or is "every creature" really meant in Revelation 5:13 as St John describes the worship of God from "every creature which is in heaven and on the earth and under the earth and such as are in the sea, and all that are in them" – obviously including the very creatures Adam is to subdue? Is it a careless generalization in both Colossians 1:23 and Mark 6:15 which speak of the Gospel being "preached to every creature"? St Francis of Assisi thought that it meant just what it said – he is described, for example, as speaking the Gospel to a flock of birds which, curiously, surrounded him.

This "dominion" then would also echo the heart-felt concern and the care of the cosmos which the daily-involved God has, of which Jesus speaks in Luke 12:6-7, 24-27:

Are not five sparrows sold for two small coins? Not one of them is forgotten before God. But the very hairs of your head are all numbered. Do not fear; you are more valuable than many sparrows. ... Consider the ravens, for they do not sow nor reap, which have no storehouse nor barn; and God feeds them. Of how much more valuable are you than the birds? ... Consider the lilies, how they grow: they do not toil nor do they spin; yet I say to you, not even Solomon in all his glory was clothed like one of these.

The "dominion" would be on-going, but also would require Adam's constant participation: new animals would be born which would need to be "subdued" and crops would have to be harvested. Perhaps in order to get water to where he wants a rice paddy, to "subdue" the earth he may need to dig irrigation ditches. Creation is "subdued" not as a battle, rather it is yielding. However the task is still work. Only after the Fall will it fight back with "thorns and thistles" [Genesis 3:18] – all those little niggling resistances that we now encounter each day, much less the big ones, like tornadoes and cancer.

Taking Over

What an awesome privilege the "subduing" and the "dominion" place upon Adam! Yet he is only the agent, "the Image and Glory of God" [I Corinthians 11:7]. Creation is not man-centric but God-centric – it exists for the sake of God's delight and enjoyment:

For in Him all things were created, in the heavens and on the earth, the visible and the invisible ... all things were created *through Him and for Him*. He is before all things, and in Him all things hold together...
                                                                            Colossians 1:16-17

The universe's value lies in the shared joy and pleasure that God takes in *all* of Creation, in His interaction with it, as indicated by *its* celebration at its birth: "When the morning stars sang together, and all the sons of God shouted for joy" [Job 38:7].[10] Adam is Jehovah's agent and partner, privileged to do those tasks that the Creator would have done by no other hands than human ones.

However, humanity has become infected with the pride and the rebellion of Satan. As Ezekiel 28:12-17 recounts, apparently "Lucifer" also had a similar privilege of representing God, in a heavenly Garden of Eden, where the scene is in crystalline material rather than plants:

> You had the seal of the full measure of wisdom and unqualified beauty. You were in Eden – the garden of God – every precious stone was your covering: ruby, topaz, diamond, beryl, onyx, jasper, sapphire, turquoise, emerald, and gold; ... You were the anointed overseeing cherub, I placed you on the holy mountain of God [often a poetic symbol for God's rule], in the settings (stones) of fire you walked. You were blameless in your ways from the day you were created, until iniquity was found in you. In the abundance of your trade [carrying God's will, carrying creation's worship] you were filled with violence/greed, and you rebelled ... Your heart was lifted up because of your beauty; your wisdom corrupted because of your splendor. ...

Satan chose instead to reflect his own heart, to be in his own "image":

> How you have fallen from the heavens, O shining star ["Lucifer"], son of the morning! You are cut down to the ground, you who weakened the nations! You have said in your heart: 'I will ascend to the heavens, I will exalt my throne above the stars of God; I will sit on the mount of assembly in the extreme north [poetic symbol of God's dwelling and rule]; I will ascend above the heights of the clouds ["clouds" is often the poetic of the vast company of angels], I will be like the Most High.
>
> Isaiah 14:12-14

Humankind's will now also echoes with this same desire to be after the Master's job, to "sit on the mount" (God's governance or dominion), emphasizing the "*I will*" – which now reflects Satan, rather than Him Who has entrusted His Creation to these agents. This rebellion, of trying to outguess and override God's will, starts in Genesis 3, and the result has been destruction and evil ever since.

The Typhoon of Sin

Creation – the "cosmos" – looks to "the Image of God" to see its beloved Creator's face and characteristics (Steadfast Love and the rest), in order to recover its balance, but something is wrong. Something has happened to "the Image." Along with "subdue," as indicated to Noah, "dominion" has become identified with "fear" and "dread."

Man looks not to the heart of God but rather into his own heart. Although created in "the Image of God" [Genesis 5:1], he fathers "a son in his own 'soul-likeness,' after his own image" [v 3]. The reflecting pool is churned up by the storm of sin. Rather than the demonstration of God's Glory, instead there is selfishness, greed, plunder, callousness, hatred and destruction. Is it any wonder that Creation has become as chaotic as the human heart? Paul identifies the situation as that

> For Creation was subjected to aimlessness and corruption, not voluntarily, but because of Him Who subjected it in hope; because the Creation also will be freed from the slavery of corruption into the freedom of the Glory of the children of God. For we know that the whole Creation groans and travails together until now. Romans 8:20-22

Man now acts as if the animals, the plants, the environment merely exist for the sake of his sport and dominance. Rather than godly-managing Creation, he would instead trophy-hunt and seek aphrodisiacs even when it means a species goes extinct. He would pollute to protect profits rather than guarantee a good environment for plant and animal. He would decimate a rainforest, rather than value its secrets[11], much less share an abundance of food with those who live there in order to maintain the precious gift that surrounds them. He would rather abort – kill – than let children cause any "discomfort" to his lifestyle or responsibilities.

> Cursed is the ground because of you; in toil (relentless struggle)[12] you shall eat of it all the days of your life. Thorns and thistles it shall bring forth to you … In the sweat of your face you shall eat bread until you return to the ground …
>
> Genesis 3:17-19

"The ground is cursed" – not by Jehovah actively cursing, but rather as the result of what we have been discussing: because of the storm of sin in the heart of the "mirror," so then nature has now become rudderless, drifting, wandering, disconnected from its Source of Life which had once been through man. Therefore, no longer a willing accomplice but rather like a hostile, even abused, child, it rebels against the rebel (man), refusing to cooperate, sabotaging his efforts, destroying his work, and demanding more time and toil to accomplish tasks.

The Restoration of "the Image"

However, as St Paul describes the situation, he includes a note of anticipation in the above Romans 8 quote. He speaks of a promise: when Jehovah allows Creation to be affected by man's sin, there is a plan *already* at work, "He chose us *in Him* before the foundation of the world" [Ephesians 1:4]. The hostility shall not always be. The cosmos will finally have its agent of God back when God's children come into their "glory," when they are "conformed to the Image of His Son" [Romans 8:29], "the Glory of Christ, Who [Himself] *is* 'the Image of God'" [II Corinthians 4:4].

Still, this will not happen by our own power – we have seen the mess we make when we go off on our own. The Holy Spirit must place us into Jesus, the only One Who could truly reflect God's Glory: "we have seen His

Glory, Glory as of the only-begotten of the Father, full of grace and truth" [John 1:14].

And now the high privilege of being God's agent is being brought back to us, as we are now entrusted with the "ministry of reconciliation; ... in Christ, God was reconciling the *cosmos* to Himself ... entrusting to us the message of reconciliation. So we are ambassadors for Christ, God making His appeal through us" [II Corinthians 5:18-20].

Having been so equipped, here indeed begins the restoring of "the Image of God" before all Creation, as Adam had first been commissioned to do, a foretaste of what Paul describes:

> Behold, I tell you a mystery: ... we all will be transformed – in a moment, in the glance of an eye, at The Last Trumpet. For the trumpet will sound, and the dead will be raised imperishable, and we shall be ... and as we have borne the image of the man of dust, we shall also bear the Image of the heavenly Man.   I Corinthians 15:51-52, 49

5. The "Helper" from God

Part of the Plan

When Jehovah creates the woman, it is no afterthought but a very deliberate step toward an important milestone in His design, just as crucial as when the man is created. She is no replacement nor a by-stander but rather a continuation of and partner in "the Image of God," with a meaningful role of her own. The high privilege of being God's "Soul-Likeness" is not duplicated but divided between them, requiring both the man and the woman in order to accomplish their remarkable shared commission. There is no competition: the unity is real, yet the roles are different.

Within this context, the man is to demonstrate the dominion of the Lord over Creation, having considerable authority yet also with significant accountability. But what is the role of the woman, her part in order to complete "the Image of God"?

The "Helper" is Who??

In Genesis 2:18, Jehovah declares that the woman would be a "helper suitable" for the man. "Helper" is an unfortunate choice for an English translation. In our modern culture, often that word indicates "an expendable assistant." In contrast, someone who has fallen down a cliff needs "a helper," but not some nonessential underling, rather a *savior* – and likely a very well-trained one – is required.

Looking at the Hebrew word for "helper," except for one instance in each of Isaiah, Ezekiel and Daniel, everywhere else in the Old Testament the word is used specifically in relation to Jehovah, and *He* is indeed by no means some "expendable assistant," but rather "Savior" is more appropriate:

> As to the source of the help, this word is generally used to designate divine aid, particularly in Psalms {Cf. Ps 121:1,2) where it includes both material and spiritual assistance. *TWOT*[13]

In Exodus 18:4 and Deuteronomy 33:7,26,29, Jehovah is a Help against enemies; a Help during times of trouble [Psalm 20:2], of stress [Psalm 33:20] and of anxiety [Psalm 70:5]; His help is reassurance [Psalm 89:19] – a *real* support [Psalm 115:9,10,11] and an effective one [Psalms 121:1,2; 124:8]; and His help is a source of confidence [Psalm 146:5] and of restoration [Hosea 13:9].

So reflecting *this* aspect of "the Image," the woman represents the very "help/saving" of God Himself to Creation (which includes her husband as part of that Creation), just as much as he demonstrates God's dominion in his management of Creation (which also includes her).

Sadly, this high office is perverted when instead of being God's "help," she tempts Adam with the forbidden fruit [Genesis 3:6]. *Yet Jehovah does not back away from His design*: in the prophecy to the serpent [v 15], it is "the woman's Seed" Who will bring about the serpent (Satan)'s destruction. Martin Luther (the 16th century reformer) once pointed out that since everywhere else in the Bible a child is "the man's seed," this wording indicates a virgin birth would produce the promised Champion for the human race – he would come solely from this "helper."

Whole Burnt Offering

Whether it be coincidence or not:

[The Hebrew] *ISHSHAH* (woman [Strong's number 802]; feminine of *ISH* – man) is the same pronunciation (although supposedly from a different root) for the *Whole Burnt Offering* [Strong's number 801] (jokes aside!!). In the woman, through whom comes temptation and through whom would come the Savior, perhaps like *oath/seven*, the ear *hears* a word directly connected with broken, restored and recommitted Covenant.

James Lindemann[14]

As an aside, to explain what the quote is talking about, "seven" is the only Hebrew number which is also a word – the word for the *oath* one makes in Covenant; in fact, the close association between the two ideas is made in Genesis 21:22-34. It is important to remember that Hebrew is more a "heard" language than one that is read. In this case it requires the listener to do a mental check to recognize which is being referred to. Even though this appears instantaneous, we know from "subliminal messaging" that even those things which the conscious mind misses are still captured in the unconscious:

A Surprising Discovery

Psychologists have discovered that the brain works faster than perhaps even it realizes. A test was once done where during a movie, a message about popcorn and soda pop was flashed for 1/3000 second every 5 seconds on the screen. Nobody noticed the additional material. Or did they? At intermission, sales of popcorn and soda pop apparently were dramatically increased during the six week period of the test. It suggests that *the brain* does indeed notice!

Subliminal [sub-conscious] stimulus or messaging by even single words has been modestly effective in changing human behavior or emotions. However its reality may have been around a lot longer than we thought.

The Case Study of Jericho

Israel stands in front of Jericho, the 'door-opener' (or the 'first-fruits,' therefore wholly dedicated to God) to the *Covenant* Land. What happens here sets the tone for the conquest of that Land which had been given by Covenant Oath to Abraham. The People, with *the Ark of the Covenant/Witness* and the *seven* priests blowing the *seven* trumpets in the center of the procession, are to encircle Jericho once each day for six days, however on the *seventh* day, *seven* times around [Joshua 6:3-20].

As the story is repeated aloud, at each 'seven,' the listeners *also* hear '[Covenant] Oath' – again and again would be the message in the background: '*Covenant* is at work – our Covenant-Partner is involved! He fights by our side!'   James Lindemann[15]

Coming back to "*ishshah*" then, as the word for "woman" or "whole burnt offering" is heard and the mind must do a quick mental flip: which is the meaning to use here? As the concept of subliminal advertising seems to indicate, even though the conscious never skips a beat, is the dual meaning something that the sub-conscious catches, a subliminal reminder that through the woman would come the promised answer to the Fall?

It does give a different perspective on Jesus' comment, "He who has ears to hear, let him hear!" [Matthew 11:15; 13:9, 43].

"Eve"

Despite the sin that has crashed in on the world and the discipline pronounced by the Lord, probably in response to the *hope* of Jehovah's promise, "Adam called his wife's name Eve [Life], because she was the mother of all living" [v 20]. What is surprising is that she is not "the mother of all humanity or humankind" but rather "of all *living*." That is the identical word in the Hebrew used in surrounding texts in the term "the *living* soul," which is applied more frequently for animals (eleven out of the first twelve instances) than for humans, as noted earlier.[16]

Why "living" rather than "humankind"? Perhaps her articulation of "the Image of God" before all Creation is to be found in her "motherhood." Indeed the epitome of her "helping/saving" will be the bearing of that Seed Who will destroy Satan, thereby bringing Life to all Creation [Romans 8:19-23] – "all living."

However, she herself is not the source of Life, nor is she the savior of Creation. It must be remembered that as "the dominion of God" is a *pass-through* authority – Jehovah's authority comes through the man but is not "owned" by him – so also is the woman's "helper/savior" role a *pass-through* status not owned by her. A mirror does not *possess* its subject, no matter how animated and life-like the image may appear. All the mirror can do is *reveal* its subject, and in essence call attention to the original. So also for those who bear "the Image," it is not by their own ability and power, but they only point to its true Subject. For example, we can be thrilled with the truly awesome honor that Mary has in bearing Jesus, however she is still only an "Image," a reflection, of the One Who saves ("God *my* Savior" [Luke 1:47]):

> ... that you may know and believe Me, and understand that I am He. Before Me was no God formed, nor shall there be after Me.
> I, I am Jehovah, and besides Me there is no savior.
> I declared, and I saved,
> I proclaimed...
> Before the day was, I am He, and no one can deliver out of My hand; I work, and who will reverse it?"
> Thus says Jehovah, your Redeemer, The Holy One of Israel ...
> Isaiah 43:10-14

The Mother

The "mother of all living" may be behind St Paul's statement to Timothy: "but she will be saved in childbearing if she continues in faith, Love, and holiness, with self–restraint" [I, 2:15]. *Strong's Exhaustive Concordance* defines the Greek word here for "childbearing" as "childbirth (parentage), i.e. (by implication) maternity (the performance of maternal duties)."[17] The word does not necessarily mean "childbirth" but may also be understood as "motherhood," so that the statement may well read, "but she will be saved in her motherhood if she continues in faith, Love, and holiness, with self–restraint."

Of course, the most immediate expression of "motherhood" springs from "childbearing," and indeed "the Image of God" has a crucial role to be played therein:

> However, this is not just about the privilege in having a pivotal role in another human's life, but also about a mother's remarkable honor of giving a child a taste of what God is like…
>
> A godly mother is right in the middle of all this. The very first experiences of love, mercy and grace will not be found in a church service, but rather right at the cradle, with the hands that clothe, feed, and rock a child. Here are lessons where words just are not enough. In the smile and the joy that the baby first recognizes, that is where the child learns about God's attitude toward him. In the plans and the promises of daily life he learns about God's intentions for him and his hope for the future. Again and again the mother's hands are a powerful tool to forge the child's coming relationship with God.
>
> James Lindemann[18]

The Mother in Nature

Here again, in the above quote, "Creation" could be substituted in place of the child with only a slight adjustment of language and it would not do much violence to the thought. "Motherhood" is not infrequently used in broader scope as well; in fact, one might wonder if "Mother Nature" and "Mother Earth" are not a corruption and distraction from the one who is to express the "motherhood," the "helper/savior" aspect of "the Image of God," to *"all living,"* that is, all Creation. Might "motherhood" cover the range from nursing a baby bird to risking one's life by aiding the wounded on a battlefield? From feeding the hungry to promoting a local arts program? From concern about the rainforest to concern about heritage and culture? Motherhood suggests a sympathizing with those unable to speak clearly for themselves; an emotional harmonizing with those who struggle with life; an educating of the fledgling.

Expanding the concept of motherhood to encompass also this more generalized aspect would then allow those who cannot have children, as well as those who choose to be celibate as Paul elsewhere encourages [I Corinthians 7:8,34], not to find themselves in an apparent disapproval from Paul's "childbearing" statement in the above I Timothy passage.

The Difference "Motherhood" Makes

So where do men come into this picture? As God directs attention to "male and female," are there not differences between them in the hearing of the ears, the seeing of the eyes, and, especially, the understandings of the heart? In an article identifying what is called "Feminine Ethics" and the viewpoint it encompasses, a contrast is made between the masculine and feminine approaches to the world:

> Fourth, traditional ethics overrates culturally masculine traits like "independence, autonomy, intellect, will, wariness, hierarchy, domination, culture, transcendence, product, asceticism, war, and death," while it underrates culturally feminine traits like "interdependence, community, connection, sharing, emotion, body, trust, absence of hierarchy, nature, immanence, process, joy, peace, and life." Fifth, and finally, it favors "male" ways of moral reasoning that emphasize rules, rights, universality, and impartiality over "female" ways of moral reasoning that emphasize relationships, responsibilities, particularity, and partiality (Jaggar, "Feminist Ethics," 1992).
>
> *Stanford Encyclopedia of Philosophy[19]*

Although not everything mentioned aligns with the original design of masculine and feminine, for example, "war, and death," still the emphasis is that her "help" brings to the table a different view of the world. She provides a holistic, subjective view which more strongly relies on the heart or emotions – the source (that is, the rib close to the heart) from which she sprang. Truly, man's expression of Jehovah's governance can indeed become focused on mechanical process, and it is important to have present the balance of these other aspects of being human.

How Come "Deceived"?

Yet in these things also lies her vulnerability. St Paul speaks of the woman as being deceived [I Timothy 2:14] – and in the Genesis account, so she is [Genesis 3:1-6,13].

Looking at the *Stanford* quote above, it is interesting that the "overrated" masculine approach emphasizes "hierarchy, domination, … rules, rights …" It must be understood that in drawing distinctions, we all tend to slightly overstate our particular case, so (hopefully) the thought in the article is not to get *rid* of these masculine qualities, but rather that they should not become the iron machine of ethics. Yet it is surprising that as one looks at the Fall into sin, these are precisely the issues which surface here with Eve. The very pivot of the account is in regard to the Creator's supremacy and a *rule*: "from 'the Tree of the Knowledge of Good and Evil' you shall not eat, for in the day that you eat from it you shall surely die" [Genesis 2:17].

Looking at the feminine ethical approach as defined in the *Stanford* quote, it is not hard to imagine how some of these "qualities," and even the discounting of the masculine characteristics, would have a part to play in Eve's decision [Genesis 3:6]. A difficulty which we have is that we can only look at this first couple from the background that is now embroiled in the rebellion of sin, along with the post-Fall apparent superiority competition between the genders. We can only *guess* as to what the qualities were like and how they would have been used before the Fall.

Satan is indeed cunning. Using the woman's qualities for his purposes, he focuses on her key role of "helper/savior" to her husband (and future family): she could improve the status of her family; they could become like God; they would not need to follow the restrictions that held them back from a supposed "better life"; they would have a world of totally new experiences. She is convinced, with all "the best of intentions," that she could "help" or "be a savior" for her family, that is, that she could "fix" their (perceived) "problem." Hence she takes of the forbidden fruit not for herself only; she also shares it with Adam.

"There is only one Savior of the world and I am not Him!" – this writer has often used this statement to remind himself when he gets too eager to fix problems by himself. After all, a mirror's subject is not itself – it rather merely reflects that which lies outside of it. So also, the woman as "God's Image" can only be dependent upon and draw attention to Jehovah, her task being that of "helping" Creation and her family to see *His* will and *His* activity in their midst through her characteristics. But this she does not do here. She totally disregards her awesome connection to the Lord, and as she promotes rebellion, rather than being the "mother of all living" she becomes the harbinger of death. The "helper/savior" has failed in her mission.

Man, the Co-Conspirator

Of course, the man is no innocent dupe – Paul declares that the man is not deceived [I Timothy 2:14], that is, he offers no protest: he does not stop the progression of sin, although he knows exactly what is going on. Both the man and the woman are equally and accountably responsible for the cataclysm of sin, suffering, and death that has since rained upon Creation.

As part of Jehovah's basis for disciplining the man, He states, "Because you have heeded the voice of your wife" [Genesis 3:17]. Some men may think this is the very reason they have been seeking when their wives accuse them of not listening, but that will not hold up under scrutiny. If she cannot be in dialogue with her husband, how then czn she carry out her role of "helper/savior"? Her role within "the Image of God" has never been rescinded, the same as the man's commission has never been cancelled.

What Jehovah is instead criticizing is that whereas the man has the ability to distinguish what is right and wrong (again refer to the *Stanford* quote) and he is *not* deceived, yet he submits to the argument of his wife even when he knows it is not the Lord's will. Therefore he has full responsibility for his rebellion. This echoes Deuteronomy 13:6-10: if family or friend attempts to lead one away from the true God, no matter how close a relationship they may have (even a *Covenant* "friend"), they are to be stoned to death.

The issue is not whether Adam should have stoned Eve, but rather that the Lord is pointing out how the capacity to judge according to God's will cannot be morally collapsed for the sake of one's emotional attachments. The man has the capacity to stop the sin right here, to "flag the play," to call for repentance and consult with the Lord – in fact, representing the Husband of Ephesians 5, He would *die* to rescue her if he could. But that does not happen here. Instead, Adam eagerly "jumps in with both feet" – apparently he has been a rebellion awaiting an occasion. Although he attempts to blame both Jehovah and his wife, ultimately it boils down to "she [merely] gave me of the tree, and I [chose to eat]" [Genesis 3:12].

As key reflections of the Creator to His Creation, this extraordinarily special pair have now obscured "the Image" – "we see as in a mirror indistinctly" [I Corinthians 13:12]. Another Savior is desperately required.

"The Helper" Comes to Save

"All flesh shall know that I, Jehovah, am your Savior and your Redeemer" [Isaiah 49:26]; "born to you this day in the city of David a Savior,

Who is Christ the Lord." [Luke 2:11]; "as also Christ is the Head of the Church and He is the Savior of the Body" [Ephesians 5:23] – in the Seed of the woman has come the perfect "Image of God," the only "Helper/Savior" that can actually rescue all of humanity, in fact, "all living," all of Creation, in their need.

His call is to turn away from rebellion, and turn to Him Who brings the full vision of God back into our world and into our lives. Through the work of the Holy Spirit, in a renewed submission to the Lord and His will, both the man and the woman will begin to recapture the awesome honor that Jehovah had planned from the beginning: that as "the Image of God" becomes more visible in the both of them, they discover their true place as representatives together of Jehovah the Creator to His Creation.

The Other Helper

> I will request from the Father, and another Helper [*Paraclete*] He will give you, Who will abide with you into eternity … But the Helper [*Paraclete*], the Holy Spirit, Whom the Father will send in My Name, that One will teach you all things, and will cause you to remember all things which I told you.   John 14:16,26

> When the Helper [*Paraclete*] comes, Whom I shall send to you from the Father, the Spirit of Truth Who goes forth from the Father, He will bear witness of Me.   John 15:26

> But I tell you the truth: it is useful for you that I go away; for if I do not go away, the Helper [*Paraclete*] will not come to you; but if I depart, I will send Him to you.   John 16:7

Humanity is not left to its own devices to wallow about in a swamp of unknowns and conjectures. There is One given to us Who will be "the Window" in that wall of the sin which prevents "the Original" from being clearly seen, Who shows Jesus and gives both the man and the woman their bearings as to what direction they are to follow. That Helper is the Holy

Spirit, the *"Paraclete"* Who is "called to the side" of one in need, Who is always at the center of those humans who want to be the reflection of "the Image of God." Without Him the task is simply impossible, the human reflection would be a pathetic caricature instead of an "Image" of real substance, and the rest of this book would not be worth the read.

The Third Helper

St Paul quotes "the marriage verse" [v 24] and tells us that it is actually is a prophecy about Jesus and His Bride, the Church.

> For we are members of His body, "of His flesh and of His bones." "For this reason a man shall leave his father and mother and shall cleave to his wife, and the two shall become one flesh" – the mystery of this is great, and I speak concerning Christ and the Church.　　　Ephesians 5:30-31

As Adam receives a new creation when Eve is born, who is appropriate for him and the task which he is to carry out, that of "Image" and "[Soul-] likeness" of God, so also, through the Holy Spirit, from Jesus' side comes a new creature, His Bride, the Church, created by "the Water" and sustained by "the Blood" [John 19:34-35; I John 5:6-8] who will be "exactly what He needs" for the task facing Him! As with Eve [Genesis 2:19-20], this new helper will be like nothing else – it will be the unique extension of Jesus, His *Body* in this world, the fulfillment of Jehovah's statement for the existence of humanity.

6. He Brought Her to the Man

"Alone" Answered by Human Covenant

In the opening scene, Jehovah declares a key characteristic about His new creature, man: "It is not good that the man should be alone" [Genesis 2:18] – that is, Adam (or *humanity*, since that is what the name also means) would be a social creature. There is a real loneliness which cannot be filled by career (as keeper of the Garden), nor by nature (when all the animals had brought to him, "there was not found a helper fit for him" [Genesis 2:20]) – loneliness is not a flaw, but rather a designed "force" which is meant to drive humans to seek out each other. Indeed, man will not be sufficient within himself, where he would need no one else – the only One who is *that* self-sufficient is the Creator.

However, remarkably, God is *also* declaring that *He* chooses to *not* be the sole sufficiency for the human either! Jehovah's plan has never been to compete with Adam's need for human companionship. His design includes neither the monastic nor the secular hermit, although there are times when, for instance, Jesus instructs His disciples to take some time out by themselves for a while [Matthew 6:31], yet never in the context of removing anyone from the companionship of fellow human beings.

As mentioned previously, "Blood/Soul/Life") provides the root word for God's "Blood-Likeness" [Genesis 1:27; 5:1], and provides the environment of the "Soul-connection" out of which Covenant with our Creator springs. As humanity reflects "the Image," then Covenant will also be part of the picture on the human-to-human level, the answer to God's declaration, "it is not good that the man should be alone."

As the man and the woman provide a binocular view of Jehovah, human-to-human Covenant also seems to be divided into two. On the one hand there is Jonathan and David's Covenant, identifying a notable example of an extraordinary human "Blood" bond between any two individuals:

> Now when [David] had finished speaking to Saul, the *Soul* of Jonathan was knit to the *Soul* of David, and Jonathan loved him as his own *Soul*. ... Then Jonathan and David cut a Covenant, because he loved him as his own *Soul*.   I Samuel 18:1, 3

Notice how "Soul" is used in the context of this Covenant, for which the practice has always been that each participant opens a wound and then mingles their Bloods (Lifes/Souls) – in the same manner as the North American First Nations practice of becoming "Blood Brothers" (or "Blood Sisters" or "Blood Brother-Sister").

It also must be mentioned that, as in the First Nations' practice, there is nothing sexual about this intense relationship. Western Culture has such poverty in the area of relationships, that it too often cannot conceive of a life-encompassing closeness without expecting it to have sexual overtones, hence the suggestion that Jonathan and David must have been homosexual. Covenant needs be reclaimed as a relationship of deepest Love *as reflecting Jehovah's Love and intimate connection to humanity,* especially as this is demonstrated by the Crown of Covenant, Jesus Himself, where *in His Person* God and Man are united by One Blood/Life/Soul. This starkly contrasts our culture's beggarly view of such relationships, and is a far cry from the usual definition of Covenant as merely a sort of legal contract. Yes, legality can have a role, but the essential core is the stated motivation for Jonathan and David's Covenant: the deep "Soul"-Love one can have for another person which is expressed in the strongest bond possible, reflecting God's "Soul"-Love for His creature, man.

The Rib

Jehovah God caused a deep sleep to fall on Adam;[20] while he slept, He took one of his ribs, and closed up its place with flesh. Jehovah God formed the rib which had taken from the man into a woman and brought her to the man.   Genesis 2:21-22

On the other hand, Covenant also has a special case in regard to marriage. The Lord begins by cutting and then removing a bone – a most unusual action for any Covenant. Yet this bone is important. Of all the 206 bones in the human body, God chooses a rib – why? A verse suggests:

Woman was not taken from man's feet that she should be his inferior,
Nor from his head that she should be his superior,
But from his side, that she should be his equal,
From under his arm, that she should be under his protection,
And from his rib, that she should be close to his heart.
                                                    various sources[21]

"Close to his heart" – Adam's strength is not in his arm as much as in his love, in his heart – the fountain of "Life-Blood." As "the Image of God," this reflects the very same center from which Jehovah operates, His Glory, especially His "Steadfast Love" [Exodus 34:6], which St Paul identifies [Romans 5:8] and St John indicates in his Gospel [3:16; 13:34] and his letters [I,3:16; I,4:17-18].

That the woman is "created" from Adam's side is not just some nice romantic thought, but this – again – is a prophecy about Jesus ("the second Adam" [I Corinthians 15:22,45]). As he "sleeps" the sleep of death on the cross, John emphasizes how from *His* side comes "the Blood and the Water" [John 19:34; I John 5:6,8]: the water of Baptism by which *His* Bride, the Church, is created, and the Blood of Holy Communion by which she is sustained in His one "Life," one "Soul."

A remarkable characteristic about ribs continues this theme: they represent restoration and regeneration. When reconstructive surgery requires bone grafts, one place to which to go is the ribs. The periosteum (the tissue sheath surrounding each rib) contains osteoblasts from which new bone grows. When this sheath is left intact and the removed piece is less than 14 cm (about 5.5 inches), the rib will be regenerated and restored (although the Creator does not need to be so limited by length). From the side of Jesus, so also is His Bride, the Church, regenerated and restored to wholeness.

That said, the language of verse 21, as it emphasizes "and closed up its place with flesh," may denote that there would be no replacement of Adam's rib.[22] Perhaps not so much to him, but at least to us, it would suggest that there would be no alternate for this woman Jehovah brings to his side. That certainly would reflect Jesus' comments in regard to divorce in Matthew 19, where He repeats the marriage verse from Genesis 2 as the context against divorce and adds, "Therefore what God has joined together, let not man separate" [v 6].

The disciples' reaction to Jesus' words is interesting: "If such is the case of the man with his wife, it is better not to marry" [v 10]. In other words, if the Covenant of marriage is so unbreakable that there be no "back door" left open, rather than commit oneself so irrevocably, it would be far better to just not get married – it would be better to avoid such a commitment, which is a surprisingly "modern" point of view. Ironically they say this to the One Who would so pledge Himself to His Bride, the Church, to "never leave [her] nor forsake [her]" [Hebrews 13:5], even when it means that "while we were enemies we were reconciled to God by the death of his Son" [Romans 5:10].

"The Womb-Man"

She shall be called "Woman," because she was taken out of "Man."

Genesis 2:23

A doctor once remarked in regard to the physical body, "There is very little difference between a man and a woman, but that difference makes all the difference in the world." The word "Woman" comes from the Anglo-Saxon "Womb-Man," which accurately reflects how the Hebrew feminine *ishah* is derived from the masculine *ish* – even our languages recognize the commonality, and the small, although never minor, differences between the two genders.[23] The female is not created separately from scratch, but rather is derived from the male, yet is not merely a man repeated.

Eve's genetic structure is basically identical to Adam's; the spiritual structure is the same; their creation identity, "the Image of God," is common between them. However, there is one important difference in this "rib" from the man's side: within the DNA, which provides the basic pattern for each individual, the "Y" (male) chromosome has been changed to a second "X" (female) chromosome in her. The result is that there is no place in a woman's body which contains a "Y" chromosome – whenever the "Y" is present, even as in the unusual case of two "X"s and a "Y", the person will *always* be a male. So, thousands of years later, when a virgin gives birth to "*her* Seed"[24] [Genesis 3:15], a *Son*, this change must be reversed – an unmistakable sign that the Creator has stepped in again to make this Birth happen.

In one respect, when Eve is created, the "Y" is just a minute chromosome which now has a second leg, and yet this miniscule difference makes "all the difference in the world." Humanity now has a "binocular" view of God, and, in her specialties of character, she will express aspects of

God that will not commonly be emphasized in the man. Although derived from a man, she is not an extension of him – her interests and concerns will often be quite different from her husband's (for example, note the difference in taste on movie night). His way and her way of doing things, seeing things, understanding things will be different – by design; both are required if we are to understand Jehovah and His Creation properly. It is also because of this that marriage encounters one of its greatest undertakings.

To Know [and Be Known]

A human yearns to be understood, not just by words, but to the depths of the Soul. St Paul identifies that this is what the Lord recognizes and seeks:

> Likewise the Spirit helps us in our weakness; for we do not know how to pray as we ought, but the Spirit Himself intercedes for us with sighs ["groanings" – KJV] too deep for words. And He who searches the hearts of men knows what is the mind of the Spirit, because the Spirit intercedes for the saints according to the will of God. Romans 8:26-27

We are well acquainted with this need. Sometimes in an argument, our struggle may not be to "win" so much as to make the other person hear what we are trying to say. We may keenly feel that we lack the words or the way to shape our thoughts so that the other person recognizes the point we are making. Of course, there are also things which are so deep inside our hearts that there *are* no words for them.

Paul says that that is a reason for the Holy Spirit's presence, so that our Lord can indeed "hear" and "understand" all that depth, even those things which have no other outlet than a sigh or a groan: extreme pain, exuberant joy, intensity of the Soul/heart's desire. When we realize that such effort to understand us has been made, and above all, that even when we are so "known," we are still not rejected, we begin to grasp just how much we are loved. (Conversely, when no real effort to listen to us is made, how unloved we can feel.) This close attention to us is the indispensable element of true intimacy, where our hearts are allowed to be "naked and not ashamed" [Genesis 2:25] to the very roots of our being, to be at one's most vulnerable to the other and still be accepted.

> O Jehovah, You know my sitting down and my rising up; You understand *my* thoughts afar off. You comprehend my path and my lying down, and are acquainted with all my ways. For there is not a word on my tongue, but behold, O Jehovah, You know it altogether. …
>
> For You formed my inward parts; You covered me in my mother's womb. I will praise You, for I am fearfully and wonderfully made; Marvelous are Your works, and that my Soul knows very well. My frame was not hidden from You, when I was made in secret, and skillfully wrought …
>
> How precious also are *Your* thoughts to me, O God! How great is the sum of them! If I should count them, they would be more in number than the sand; When I awake, I am still with You. …
>
> Search me, O God, and know my heart; Try me, and know my thoughts; and see if there is any wicked way in me; lead me in the way everlasting. Psalm 139:1-4, 13-15, 17-18, 23-24

Once this sinks in, that Jehovah would know us to this intimate degree, it is an awesome thing. But what is startling is that He desires this intimacy to be reciprocal:

> I will betroth you to Me forever; yes, I will betroth you to Me in righteousness and justice, in Steadfast Love and mercy; I will betroth you to Me in faithfulness, and you shall *know* Jehovah. Hosea 2:19-20

There is more at work here than merely the *reflection* of "the Image of God" – we *participate* in the intimacy! Not only is the human "known" by God, but God is to be "known" by the human. His understanding is so encompassing and profound, touching with His Spirit the hidden places of our hearts, even those areas of which we ourselves may barely be aware.

And yet the Lord is determined to "expose" Himself, to be vulnerable, to be "naked and not ashamed." Again St Paul's words in Ephesians 3:

> that you, being rooted and grounded in love, may be able to comprehend with all the saints what is the width and length and depth and height – to know the Love of Christ which passes knowledge; that you may be filled with all the fullness of God.   Ephesians 3:16-19

Therefore He has given us "the diary of His heart and mind," the Bible, so that we might see Him in action. We discover the great Love in His gift of Christmas, His absolute commitment on the Cross, and His tenacious hope in His Resurrection. The more we read and study His Word, the more we see Him binding Himself in Covenant to humans, the more we see the humanity of Jesus, the more we can say that we *know* Who He is, and with Whom we are dealing.

In the midst of the "knowing and being known" in which we participate, we now are reflecting it, especially in the one-to-one relationship of marriage. This is hard work: our human material is so very limited in its abilities to mirror this intimacy with God, and attempting such a deep mutual understanding is very demanding. That is why His design for marriage narrows the scope to only one man and only one woman – it takes undivided concentration to do the careful listening which intimacy requires.

Within the *marriage* context, there is a highly symbolic act, a *communication* which goes beyond words, which opens a door to the very core of oneself. In an environment of mercy, grace, faithfulness, forgiveness and Love – a reflection of God's Glory – it involves the exploration into the personhood of each other, and risking the exposure of oneself in return.

Is it of any surprise then that both the Old and the New Testaments would use the verb "to know [and be known]" to describe this very act? What we ignore is that the act of sex in the human is specially crafted to be such a *dialogue* (which is what "intercourse" actually means) in which, expressed beyond words, are the deep things of one's heart revealed to the other. Beyond idealism, this intimacy then takes concrete form in a child – *there* is to be the evidence of the unity that they have been cultivating.

Sadly, this design which is meant for the understanding, acceptance and faithfulness of the heart has been rejected and the mechanics are pushed to center stage. This act "to know [and be known]" is now seen as merely self-gratifying recreation; or it is used as a weapon of power or of manipulation. Is it any surprise that the majority of a thesaurus' alternatives for "intimacy" are merely descriptions of the sexual act? There are very few, if any, suggestions in regard to the mutual heart knowledge shared between two people.

God's Exact Solution

When Covenant is broken, like an animal torn in half, all that is left are two dead pieces with the "Life-Blood" drained away. However, what happens at Eve's creation is not death but expanded Life. It begins, as it were, with Covenant in mirror action: not two persons joined into one, rather from one, *two living persons* share the same Blood, that is, the same "Soul" and "Life," the same chromosomes, the same task of reflecting "the Image," and more.

As Jehovah puts the hand of the woman into the hand of the man, He identifies that this new creature is exactly what the man *needs*: the fitting answer to his aloneness, the ideal solution to his empty spaces, the perfect complement to share in his life, work, and responsibilities. He responds:

This is now bone of my bones and flesh of my flesh   Genesis 2:23

There is a concrete sense to this. "My bone" and "my flesh" describe a real, personal and physical connection, as is indicated in other passages where these words are used [for example, Genesis 29:14 and II Samuel 5:1]. It is the recognition of the joint origin and the common purpose of existence, as well as of companionship.

Although this woman is exactly what the man *needs*, she may not necessarily be what he *wants*. Sometimes we want someone who is an extension of ourselves, of our perspectives and of our opinions. We may have fantasies about what the spouse *ought* to be, but often those fantasies are not healthy for us – sometimes he/she may need to walk us into the harsh light of reality. There are times when the Lord must teach us something which may be unpleasant.. Consider the options: He can use our spouse, or someone who does not love us like our spouse does. We can either "shoot the messenger" or appreciate, respect and listen to God's choice of teacher. Before we get into whatever the argument may be, consider whether the Lord is using our spouse as the last chance to have someone who loves us be His guide to us.

Having divided the one into two, and now bringing the two to be joined as one in the marriage Covenant, this is indeed "a reuniting." Truly, Jehovah did bring Adam and his wife together, with the realization that "nothing ever happens by coincidence." The Creator is involved and it is His delight to bring happiness into those who are His Covenant-partners.

As He holds each one's hands, there is a trinity here as well. Such a marriage has been described as a triangle, which is the strongest, most unbreakable of all shapes that we have. The Base is God's presence and working throughout the marriage, and each partner joins to form a structure that will not be crushed by the world and the circumstances of life, while in the well-protected center are the children.

"Or Do We Look For Another?"

Yet there is danger here as well. The media loves to accent the romantic ideals of "marriages made in heaven," "the soul-mate," and "there is only one person in the world created for me." Two people "click" together or "zing!" from the moment they meet, and the impression is that this should be *the* way things are done.

That would be so nice! It would then take the difficult decision process out of our hands. We would not have to struggle to learn about our future mate, testing whether we can truly work together, value each other, enjoy each other. To expect such automatic recognition to happen is to take what should be a dynamic relationship and expect a mechanical, surprisingly dull, ready-made result, with no real work required. Sure, it is so wonderful at the beginning, but unfortunately the work of "to know [and be known]" will still be required for the duration of the marriage. It will take effort in order to maintain and enhance this bond, especially when the routines, and perhaps the drudgery, of daily existence seek to take the life out of the relationship.

This becomes particularly evident when we experience the agony of second-guessing our choice of mate, particularly if it depended on such a "zing!" experience. The idea of only one person created for us can leave us wondering whether or not the spouse we have is really "that One, or should we be looking for another?" [Luke 7:19, 20]. Although John the Baptist asks that question in a vastly different context, it is useful to look at this incident for the moment.

At this point in John's life, conditions are dismal – an outdoorsman to the hilt, he is in a hole in the ground which is the prison of the day [Luke 3:19-20], awaiting death [Matthew 14:1-12]. He becomes disheartened, and begins to question whether Jesus really is the awaited Messiah, which is surprising since he had been so definite when Jesus came earlier to be baptized by him [John 1:29-36].

Jesus' answer is a useful one for us as well. At first He says little, knowing that mere words often give hollow reassurance. He simply lets John's disciples observe the things he does – healings, casting out demons, teaching [vv 21-23]; then He identifies that these actions are John's answer – unmistakable trustworthy evidence which gives solid confidence.

It is in concrete experience, not in glossy romantic idealism, that their – and our – proof lies. Only this type of grounding for our faith – in the Lord and in each other – can sustain us when we are assailed by doubts.

Simply put, Jesus' answer – and ours here, too – is to "stop looking!" Leaving open the back door of doubt simply weakens one's commitment to, and focus on, this marriage Covenant. When we make our choice, we must establish the proofs – not the "zing!" – which will help us weather the times of doubt. Our energy for each other gets sapped away as we continually evaluate each "new prospect," as we constantly judge our mate against the façade and imagined qualities of that new "answer to our yearnings." Instead, once God brings us together at the altar in marriage, as the vows put it, "forsaking all others, keep yourself for her/him only."

How Does One Know?

"Oh, you will just know when the right one comes along" – there probably are no more frustrating, empty and useless words that could be spoken when attempting to determine who will be one's life-mate. Yes, there will be strong attraction, and yes, there can be deep commonality with that person. But when looking to spend the rest of a life together that touches on eternity, is this really enough?

Perhaps Jesus' answer to John has value even here at this beginning point of the relationship.

> [Jesus] answered them, "Go and report to John what you have seen and heard: the blind receive their sight, the lame walk, lepers are cleansed, the deaf hear, the dead are raised, the poor are given the Good News, and blessed is he who is not offended by Me."   Luke 7:22-23

No, we are not looking for a miracle worker – or perhaps we are (although not at Jesus' level).   Does the potential mate bring new perspectives – new sight – to us? Do we have ability to move about in areas in which we only limped before? Do we find the untouchable (leprous) areas of ourselves cleansed? Do we hear with more understanding? What has been made alive in us because of the experience of knowing this other person? Beyond the romantic rose-colored glasses, what is it which we most highly value? It must be kept in mind that all these things are what we want to build a *lifetime* upon, not just what excites us for the moment. What will be left, once the normalcy of life begins to take over, as it will since we physically cannot run on high excitement for extended periods of time?

And especially, how about the "Good News" and no offense? The "Good News" ("Gospel") in the Bible is specifically a reference to Jesus and His work, along with the love, hope and life that comes through His forgiveness won on the cross – these things center on one's relationship to the Creator, beyond the more commonplace aspects of life. The question is whether the prospective mate is able to bring the "Good News" to us, since this provides the relationship's concrete platform of love, mercy, grace, faithfulness, forgiveness – the Glory of God – the reflection of "the Image," and solid hope.

This is by no means trivial. Samuel Clemens (Mark Twain) fell in love and married a Christian girl named Livy (Olivia). She was devoted to God and wanted her family to be also. She insisted on prayers at mealtimes and set up a family altar to have spiritual devotions each day. One day Sam said, "Livy, you go on with this by yourself if you want, but leave me out. I don't believe in your God and you're only making a hypocrite out of me." As time passed, Livy fell further and further from God. When the crisis of the death of two of their three grown daughters and Livy's own impending death came, Sam said to her, "Livy, if your Christian faith can help you now, turn to it." She replied, "I can't, Sam, I have none left. It was destroyed a long time ago."[25] Rather than having a "Good News" with which to support each other in a time of great need, instead there was "none left," leaving behind a hopelessness that both felt.

Since the decision for a lifetime mate has eternal ramifications, it is not casual, but must be done with a measured step of discovery combined with thoughtful wisdom.

7. The Marriage Covenant

Therefore a man leaves his father and his mother and cleaves to his wife, and they become one flesh.

Genesis 2:24

Leave

Such exclusivity! Whenever this Hebrew word for "leave" appears, two-thirds of the time it is translated as "forsake." The concept is very strong: one's other primary relationships are to be "forsaken." Obviously this does not mean that one ceases to have any friends or family, rather that they are at best to take second place – even Covenants with other people are not to interfere with *this* bond. Likewise in the command to honor father and mother, obedience to them no longer applies (although the love and care for the parents are to continue [I Timothy 5:8; II Corinthians 12:14]).

A new family unit has emerged that has a special role within "the Image of God." The Creator's intent was never to compete with the need for human companionship; instead His design has always been a "both-and" unity of Himself and the couple – they are to provide the dual perspective on "the Image of God," and He will be their Source and Protector for this bond:

> ... for [Jehovah] does not regard the offering, nor receive it with delight from your hands. And you ask, "Why?" Because Jehovah has been witness between you and the wife of your youth, against whom you have dealt deceitfully, yet she is your companion and the wife of your Covenant! Did He not make them one, who has a remnant of the Spirit? Why one? He was seeking offspring for God. So guard your spirit and do not deal deceitfully with the wife of your youth!
>
> Malachi 2:13-15

Jehovah from the beginning refused to fill the loneliness for which only another human (for the single, some other important person(s) in one's life) is to answer. His intent is not to compete with human community – He creates it!

Unfortunately, because of humanity's rejection of its Creator, there are times when "either-or" dilemmas occur, when humans attempt to pit particularly the marriage relationship against the Lord, "It's either me or God." This can happen fairly frequently, as when a person belittles and discourages a spouse's involvement in their faith and commitment. An example, mentioned above, is Samuel Clemens (Mark Twain) with his often scathing opinion of Christianity, and how it decimated his wife Livy's faith over time, until she "had none left." There are instances where a husband in essence forbids his wife from any activity in church, perhaps scheduling activities that will deliberately conflict even with worship. Wives also have done the same to the husband. Some cults encourage their women as their "sacrifice" to marry Christian men, then use the marriage as leverage to persuade the men to leave their faith and to join "the church."

So when such a conflict is imposed, Jesus has harsh words for those who want to force the fight: "If anyone comes to Me and does not hate his father and mother, wife and children, brothers and sisters, yes, and his own life also, he cannot be My disciple" [Luke 14:26]. Just like "forsake," "hate" is a deliberate overstatement meant to highlight that, as "the Image of God," if one is to reflect the Lord, then the mirror cannot be turned toward anything else. Anything else that lays claim to our lives merely results in an ultimate emptiness and less than fulfilling purpose to existence. Another example is Deuteronomy 13:6-10, which has hard words when a brother, son, daughter, spouse or (Covenant) friend tries to seduce us away from following the true God.

Cleave

When an unclean spirit goes out of a man, it goes through waterless places, seeking rest, and finds none. Then it says, 'I will return to my house out of which I came.' When it comes, it finds [the place] idle (unoccupied), swept, and decorated (prepared)[26]. So it goes and takes with it seven other spirits more evil than itself, and they enter and dwell there; and the last state of that man is worse than the first. So shall it also be with this wicked generation.   Matthew 12:43-45

Although it may be puzzling to use this passage in relation to the marriage verse, the point which Jesus makes is that merely getting rid of something ("empty") does not solve a spiritual problem. Something else must fill the vacuum or else the end result is far worse than the original condition. For example, there are some who are so preoccupied with using marriage as the opportunity of getting away from their parents ("leaving"), that if this is their basic motivation, then it can too easily become a case of "the last state ... is worse than the first."

"Leave" and "cleave" must work side-by-side with each other – on one hand there is the constant turning away from whatever may affect the intimacy and oneness of the relationship, while on the other hand there must be a deliberate commitment to build up this significant bond. Ultimately the two are to reflect "the Image of God" to each other, in which they are determined to exhibit "the Glory of God" – those attributes of grace, mercy, Steadfast Love, faithfulness, forgiveness and the rest – and thereby reflect to their children, to others and to Creation that extraordinary Covenant in which God would "superglue" Himself to those who would be His Bride, His People:

Who shall separate us from the Love of Christ? Shall tribulation, or distress, or persecution, or famine, or nakedness, or danger, or sword? ... For I am confident that neither death, nor life, nor angels nor principalities nor powers, nor what is present, nor what is coming, nor height nor depth, nor any other created thing, will be able to separate us from the Love of God in Christ Jesus, the Lord of us.

Romans 8:35,38-39

"Nothing shall separate": Reflecting this bond, nobody and nothing will come between the spouses. Each will stand up for the other. Neither will speak negatively about the other,. Neither will tolerate anyone talking against the spouse. There will be no "complaint orgies" with friends. Once in a magazine article a couple reflected on how they kept saying in their conflicts, "How can we go on like this?", until they finally believed that message. Sadly, after their divorce, they realized that nothing which they faced had been that insurmountable – they had merely convinced themselves that there was no way to deal with their differences No, "nor any other created thing" is to come between the spouses – not money, work, children, nor anything else.

However, "the man" and "the woman" are still individually to reflect "the Image of God" – their various responsibilities are neither to be neglected nor abolished. Rather, their unity further equips them to carry out their commission and commitments *together* within their joint binocular expression of God's Glory in this world.

"I Plight Thee My Troth"

Marriage has been described as "a need-meeting arrangement." Yet the vow is not "I demand you pledge yourself to me," but rather "I pledge my true Love and all which I am *to you*," as is declared in the older versions of the wedding service. This is what is meant in the words which the man repeated, "thereto I plight thee my troth" or in more contemporary English, "therefore I pledge to you my truth [or fidelity]," in response to his vow to love, comfort, honor, and keep her … for better for worse, for richer for poorer, in sickness and in health, to love and to cherish, till death us do part, according to God's holy ordinance.[27]

More than merely words, this is the pledge to *nourish* love, to keep it alive and well in all circumstances. Therefore the man puts his whole honor, dignity, character and trustworthiness at stake on this. Unfortunately these qualities are not as highly regarded today as they were then.

Again this only reflects Jehovah's greater commitment in Covenant to His People. Turning again to Hosea 2:19-20, most translations agree that "troth" or "betroth" is the fitting meaning for the Hebrew word in:

I will *betroth* you to Me forever; I will *betroth* you to Me in righteousness and justice, in Steadfast Love *[HESED]* and compassion; I will *betroth* you to Me in faithfulness, and you shall know Jehovah.

Although it is most visible in regard to marriage, this is actually the nature of all Covenants: they declare not only what is but also what will be brought into existence. One comes across attempts to change the marriage ceremony so that the "vow" is merely a profession of love, but a vow is not a mere statement of status at the moment, rather it reflects a measured decision and commitment to invest one's self into what this bond could and should be "till death do us part." It is the pledge to be dependable and accountable no matter what the circumstances.

It is the determination to truly reflect "the Image" to the opposite gender, demonstrating in real life God's commitment to us. Not just an example or a model, Jehovah is an *active* participant – the Glue – Who gives hope, strength, forgiveness, perspective, stamina, and so much more, especially a Steadfast Love; pouring these qualities out into the heart of each participant [Romans 5:1-5], and then through each to the other. As mentioned above in regard to Romans 8, this Love will not be thwarted by any circumstance: "nothing will stop me from loving you, even if you do not return the affection in the same way or to the same extent!" In the following verses in Romans 5, this expression of Love would still hold even if the other is an "enemy" [v 10].

In dramatic contrast to the world's concepts of love which range from excitement-oriented, recreational sex to the casual game of self-centered love, or to the intensely-selfish possessive love; instead of the steadfast, determined, unconditionally-giving, thou-centered Love of God upon which the vows focus. This is no fantasy love, but rather the commitment to share together all the realities of life, "for better for worse, for richer for poorer, in sickness and in health, to love and to cherish." Of course, we will never fully reflect how God cleaves to us, but the vows indicate that we will strive to make it as close to a reality as we can.

Truly, romantic love is not enough on which to build a marriage, but neither should it be discounted, since it has the capacity to cut through the flaws of a person to glimpse the Creator's vision of him/her, His "Image." This in turn compels us to visualize of what could be and what we are work toward in the relationship; to see what is priceless and extraordinary in each other; and to renew the delight, the joy, the excitement, and even the play which Love encompasses. Although it may occupy a smaller percentage of a couple's relationship as time goes on, such romantic love should never disappear from it.

Steadfast Love

Jesus cleaves to His Bride. Those words sound so casual, but they encompass a great deal. Cleaving to His Bride has not been easy for Him. Not only did He give of Himself on the Cross, to this day, Jesus is still giving of Himself totally. He is giving His very own Flesh and Blood, still leaving His Father on high to spend one-to-one time with His Bride, giving of

Himself Body, Soul, and Spirit. That is what John chapter 6 declares as to what His commitment requires.

In verse 66, we see many of His disciples walk out on Jesus – they do not want such a relationship. After all, if God the Son would give Himself to such a degree, then they also are called upon to give themselves equally so to Him, Body, Soul, and Spirit. The message challenges human nature.

Yet Jesus continues to cleave to His wife, even when she has walked out on Him, even when she has turned her back on Him, even though she does not trust Him and does not understand Him, He continues to be faithful despite how it ultimately costs His life.

How unlike us that is! We would demand, force, control; some might even beat upon the spouse. But Jesus simply cleaves to His wife, supporting, nurturing, assisting, listening – giving of Himself totally to His Bride (us!) constantly. He is disgraced and abused, ignored and even held up to ridicule, yet He stands waiting for His Bride to come back to Him because He has made her so valuable to Himself. This is what Jesus would do for those who have rejected Him, who count themselves as enemies of God [Romans 5:8-11].

But for those who turn to Him, this is a commitment which will reach beyond death, all the way into new and eternal life.

One Flesh

Strong's *Hebrew Lexicon* says that the Hebrew word for "flesh" can also mean "body" and by extension "person,"[28] so that the passage means that upon the foundation of the "leaving" and the "cleaving," the two now are to become one person – which is Covenant language, a marriage-Covenant. They are united, not just in regard to their relationship with each other, but also as "the Image of God" and as the High Priest of Creation. There is a uniqueness here as compared to its reflected companion-Covenant, such as Jonathan and David's bond.

Although both types of Covenants have similarity in answer to God's declaration, "It is not good that the man should be alone," yet the "one flesh" of marriage has the distinctive "binocular" perspective. As well, in its unique language of the heart and Soul, the sexual dialogue provides the "one flesh/one person" a concrete and tangible expression in the oneness of a child. Here is the consequence of the vow which declares not only what is, but also "what will be brought into existence."

The One "Real" Marriage

In Paul's famous (and to some, infamous) section on marriage in Ephesians, He quotes the marriage verse from Genesis 2 and then adds, "This mystery is a profound one, and I am saying that it refers to Christ and the Church" [Ephesians 5:32]. In other words, to really understand marriage in Genesis, we have to look to *the opposite end* of history at the relationship of the Lamb (Jesus) and His Bride (the Church) [Revelation 21:9] – this is the key to unlock about what human marriage is about, especially Adam and Eve's in their sinless state.

The first marriage then would not be the ultimate defining example, but is merely *the reflection and prophecy* of the final one, the heavenly Marriage. Should this surprise us? Not really, because the stated reason for human existence all along has been how humanity is to reflect "the Original" as "the Image of God." The Marriage of "Christ and the Church" is not based on human versions, but rather it is the other way around: what defines all marriages is the Bridegroom's one perfect eternal union with His Bride. Paul carefully identifies the husband's and the wife's roles, not as what they *should* be, but rather what they already are within the "Original" version *which exists in eternity.*

Indeed, Paul is correct! Genesis 2:24 does describe Jesus: this Man left His Father and the majesty of Heaven, He "'neutralized' Himself, taking the nature of a slave, having become the likeness of men" [Philippians 2:7]; He left His mother, distancing Himself from her at the Wedding of Cana [John 2:4] as He begins His ministry – the wooing of His Intended; He cleaves to His Wife, the Church, "Never will I leave you, never will I forsake you" [Hebrews 13:5]; and He and His Bride, the Church, become one Flesh, one Body, one Person.

The Ceremony

A friend once asked if there is any Biblical requirement for a wedding *ceremony* – why does "just living together" not simply and more cheaply "do the job"?

One reason in answer is that human marriage is to reflect the "Original" marriage and heaven is described as a *wedding feast (ceremony)* between Jesus and His Bride:

> I heard, as if the sound of a great crowd, as if the sound of many waters and as if the sound of mighty thunders, saying, "Alleluia! Since the Lord God Omnipotent reigns, let us rejoice and jump for joy and give the Glory to Him, because the marriage of the Lamb is come, and His Wife has made herself ready." To her it was given that she be clothed in fine linen, unblemished and bright, for the fine linen is the righteousness of the saints.
> Then he said to me, "Write: 'Blessed are those who are called to the Supper of the Marriage of the Lamb!'" ...   Revelation 19:6-9

Other examples are the parables in Matthew 22:2-14 (the guests who refused to come to the wedding) and Matthew 25:1-13 (the Ten Virgins).

In Malachi 2:13-15 quoted earlier, Jehovah calls marriage a Covenant, and one does not "fall" into Covenant – it requires a ceremony, where vows declare an explicit declaration of self-commitment. This relationship cannot be private since it affects the life of the whole community; it is not whispered love, but love made known before God and community. It provides the fence to give the freedom, the climate where the couple can enjoy each other in his and her full personhood.

As mentioned, the vows are not merely a statement of status. They look deliberately toward the future as to what effect this Covenant will have for the couple "till death do us part." They declare that they will not shatter as the relationship is constantly readjusted by life circumstances: there will be the framework to confront problems; there will be the trusting environment in which to discover the depths of each other:

> and again, Eph 5, what Paul is saying is not that the marriage of the Lamb is like human marriage. What Paul is saying is that there is no marriage outside the marriage of the Lamb – that is THE marriage. Once that is established, now human marriage is the earthly representation of the eternal thing, but only after establishing that the Lamb's marriage is THE marriage. This makes human marriage a very, very important event/relationship because it must, it can only, it has to describe in earthly terms a heavenly, hence the only, reality. A common law relationship has no commitment – already there is a distortion of THE marriage.
>
> ... you say that they have entered common law by choice – not really. There is not the choice as when one is willing to commit self totally for better, for worse, to the death, as Jesus did for His Bride, and as the Bride is willing for her Husband. Common law is entered in, as opposed to the ceremony, because one wants to always leave a back-door open. Hence it is impossible to fully give of oneself when there is always the sense that "but if this doesn't work out, I can always leave."
>
> ... if you are willing to make the definitive commitment, then why common-law? Why not make the commitment, where you declare before the world that you give of yourself totally? If you are unwilling to do that, then you are hedging; if you are hedging, you are leaving a back-door open; if you are leaving a back-door open, then you are not

committing yourself as Christ did, and as the Church is to Him; then you are NOT representing the marriage of the Lamb! After all, Jesus was willing to declare His total commitment; …[29]

In addition to this, the ceremony fulfills a community role, particularly in the "leaving" and "cleaving": on one hand, it is the declaration to all that they may no longer view the couple as "the son of …" or "the daughter of …," but from now on, "the spouse of …" (which is the "leaving" aspect); on the other hand, it gives the community the chance to commit whatever resources it can to help the couple maintain their unity (the "cleaving" aspect), especially as it is the signal telling all other "possible suitors" "hands off!" this couple.

The "Original" "One Flesh" Concept

The difficulty here is that a mirror cannot reveal the fullness of the object it reflects, but rather is limited by its own material, even when the "mirror" is a special creation by God. The idea of "oneness" between Christ and His Bride has a breathtaking richness:

> His divine power has granted to us all things that belong to Life (that is, Jesus) and godliness, through the knowledge of Him Who called us to His own Glory and excellence, through which He has given to us His precious and very great promises, that through these you might be partakers (*koinonia*) of the Divine Nature …   II Peter 1:3-4

The extent of the oneness is that we "might be partakers of the divine nature"! The Greek word "partaker" [*koinonia* – participation/communion] is echoed in Paul's statement in regard to Holy Communion in I Corinthians 10:16:

> The Cup of Blessing which we bless, is it not a *participation* in Christ's Blood?
> The Bread which we break, is it not a *participation* in Christ's Body?

And even Jesus declares, "He who eats My Flesh and drinks My Blood abides in Me, and I in him" [John 6:56], expressing (as best as human words can get it) the full two-way street of oneness which He has with His Bride as demonstrated in the act of Holy Communion. The Bridegroom, in unparalleled life-giving love, gives His very self to His Bride: *His Divine Nature* enters her, becomes one with her, she lives in Him, He lives in her [John 15:4] – His Church truly becomes one Body with Jesus, "the Body of Christ":

> "Body of Christ" is an extraordinary expression. It is without parallel even in the Old Testament. Seneca, to be sure, was quite ready to refer to the citizens of Rome as a body politic. We are quite familiar with terms "student body" or "church body." To speak of church members as a body of Christians creates no particular excitement. However, that is not what the apostle chose to write. He spoke of Christians as the "body of Christ." That is to say, in some mysterious sense the church is an extension of the incarnation of our Lord. It does His work. It is His instrument within history to carry on Christ's mission of gathering all things under His lordship. Dr Martin H Scharlemann[30]

The impact of Dr Scharlemann's point is reflected in I Corinthians 12:12:

> For just as the [human] body is one and has many members, and all the members of the body, being many, are one body, so also is Christ.

Paul does not say, "so it is with Christ and the Church," or "Christ and believers," but rather, simply, "Christ." This is the extent of the oneness: to Paul, apparently, "Christ" does not refer to just Jesus, but also *must* include His entire Body – all believers – Head and Body always as an undivided, seamless whole, the ultimate in cleaving to His Wife – after all, they are one Flesh, one Body, one Person..

What an awe-filled picture this is! But now, how can the human marriage reflect this astonishing concept of this Creator-creature oneness?

Sexual Intercourse

On this basis, we must start with the "Original" and then ask what the reflection, within its limitations, is trying to show us. If we treat what Jehovah is doing as a reflection of the human relationship, which is what some religions attempt to do, the result is a grotesque and repulsive caricature of His connection with us. Instead, the human sexual relationship, in its meager and inexact way, attempts to alert us concerning the "One Flesh" unity of Jesus with His Church.

In Jesus' declaration "This is My Body, This is My Blood," we see Him earnestly, delightedly, boldly, actually, giving Himself "Flesh and Soul" (Body and Blood) – literally everything He is and has, holding back nothing – to His Bride, seeking her contentment in His love, and desiring that she would give nothing less than *her* whole self in return. This Sacrament is a powerful expression of God's commitment, Steadfast Love, and the intimacy of His heart, indeed to the degree "that through these you may be partakers of the divine nature" [II Peter 1:4].

Therefore, as has been emphasized, the essential message of the human relationship is simply to be a glimpse of that much greater oneness between Jesus and His Church. With the humans, not only is there the union of two Bodies, but also of two Souls within their emotional, intellectual and social capacity, and especially of their two Spirits in their capacity to reflect the oneness into which God places us. Sadly, our modern culture focuses on the mechanics of the sexual act and on one's own gratification – a by-product of the selfishness of sin – rather than to realize how this should humbly reflect God's extreme heart-felt and Steadfast Love which begins in Bethlehem with the birth of Jesus and reaches its most profound self-giving moment on the Cross.

A major problem arises when one is not connected with the Lord. Spiritually that person is without Life, which means that as "good" as the sex may be, there cannot be any spiritual unity. There will not be the unity of Life and the reflection of "the Image" just cannot take place – their spiritual identity and purpose of life is without anchor.

But when this type of self-giving by the humans is the reflection of their connection to Jesus, then the new life (child) which can result becomes a beautiful expression of His gift of Life to His People, the Church. Because of who "the man" and "the woman" are, as the "Image" and "Likeness" of God, then sexual intercourse is not mere animal behavior, but it is transformed into a dramatic reflection of Jehovah's total giving of Himself on behalf of His Beloved – not just to the humans but also to all Creation.

No Longer Alone

In answer to the statement, "It is not good that the man should be alone," all that "the Image of God" can do is to reflect the Original, in two ways. On the one hand is the powerful Covenant which echoes Jehovah's extraordinarily close relationship as, for example, between Abraham and Himself (between human and Divine), which we then see between Jonathan and David (between human and human). On the other hand, there is the dramatic Covenant found between the eternal Bridegroom with His Blood-redeemed Bride, which we then see in the marriage of Adam and Eve (between "male and female"). The result is that humankind is placed into vertical and horizontal Covenants, into vertical and horizontal relationships.

Right from the beginning, but especially in the united commission of "the man" and "the woman," a very distinctive significance is given in their reflecting God. Therefore in their dual-gender – binocular – view, Creation would have an on-going demonstration of its Creator.

84

Sadly, sin has misshapen this picture terribly. It has been broken in so many ways, even more so in our contemporary culture which treats such unity as interfering in its sexual self-gratification. Yet any solution aside from what God intends merely brings about a certain hollowness to life, as the Creator's stated reason for each gender's existence is discarded. The real satisfaction of understanding our place in Creation and of discovering how crucial we are in God's partnership in His dealings in the universe is snubbed. We fail to appreciate, much less to know, the extreme honor placed on us, and without that most of what we do on earth is ultimately meaningless.

We are called to repent of our turning away from Jehovah's design, and through His forgiveness to discover the vision that He has always had about our significance in this and in the coming world. His desire in sending Jesus to the Cross on our behalf is to move us closer to being what He declared us to be from the very creation of humankind. With the presence of the Holy Spirit given to us according to His promises, we can delve into the oneness that He seeks with us, and to practice the oneness that He gives between us and our spouses. Here awaits us the adventure, not always easy, of being "the Image of God" in a Covenant of the oneness of "Soul" and of "Life" between "the man" and "the woman."

8. Submission

Them's Fighting Words!

In Ephesians 5, St Paul instructs:

> Wives, submit to your own husbands as to the Lord, for the husband is head of the wife, as Christ is Head of the Church; and He is the Savior of the Body.
>
> vv 22-23

Submit?? How dare Paul make such a suggestion! It means that the wife must make herself vulnerable to her husband, and that just is not fair. It could even be dangerous!

But Paul is not merely making idle talk. Dismissing him as anti-feminist does not fit what he is doing – he is simply looking at the "Original" Marriage of Jesus with His Bride, and then identifying what we are to be about if we are truly reflecting "the Image." It is one of the areas of our relationship with God which challenges our human nature.

Besides, what is most often missed when one looks from a prejudiced judgment is that Paul's view is far more encompassing – for instance, he uses the *same* word "submit" just one verse prior, when he instructs *everyone* (at least among Christians):

> Submit to one another out of reverence for Christ.
>
> v 21

Does he mean that even *the men* are under his instruction to submit? But is not the man "the head," the boss of the family? Is not "submit" the opposite of "subdue and have dominion," which is the man's task? However, consider what Paul says in I Corinthians 7:

To the wife, the husband must give the debt/obligation due her, and likewise the wife to the husband. The wife does not have authority over her own body, but the husband does; and likewise the husband does not have authority over his own body, but the wife does. vv 3-4

This mutual submission really irks our human nature – now *everybody* should be mad at Paul! How dare he say that any of us is to submit to another human being!

Trust is the Problem

In premarital discussions concerning God's blueprint for marriage, this idea of submission often meets strong reaction. There is an attitude of distrust. This is curious since marriage involves the mutual pledging of each's whole life to the other "'till death do we part," and yet there is the sense that "but to dare to *really* commit myself *that totally* to you – no, I cannot trust you, I must hold back, I must protect myself." After all, the depth of this commitment goes to the core of one's being – "bone of my bone and flesh of my flesh" is how Adam put it – and that is distressingly comprehensive to simply hand over to anyone else.

But if one cannot trust the other person, then why get married? Why go through the motions of pledging one's life to a person who cannot be trusted completely with the most valuable thing (one's self) which anyone can have? But what if the inner character of the other is not known well enough to be given such a trust? Then why would a relationship which *requires* such a degree of commitment to each other be rushed into? The purpose of courtship is not so much to have a guaranteed weekend date and fun times, but to spend the time getting past the novelty and discovering the person to whom will be surrendered the next possibly fifty years – often twice the ages of the marrying couple.

In addition, if there is no common respect for the Lord and for each other's relationship to Him as the foundation for such mutual trust, then the script is most vulnerable for the ending to turn out very badly.

"Living together" in a common law relationship is even worse – this is a false relationship, attempting to have the benefits without the commitment, without the core, "bone and flesh," being involved. Yet the human isn't built that way, since the reality is that one *does* hand over one's self to the other, yet without any of the safeguards, without the honest evaluation and commitment that a marriage calls for. The "safety" valve of leaving "the backdoor" open for a quick escape simply does not compare to the real "safety" of two people pledged to their common task of "knowing and being known," and of reflecting together, and to each other, "the Image" of that God Whom they so desire the world should see in them. This commitment is no casual temporary promise, but rather that which defines and shapes the basic person for each spouse, and that is why God abhors the idea of cutting this bond:

> For Jehovah God of Israel says He hates divorce, for it covers one's garment with violence. Jehovah of Hosts says therefore to keep watch over your spirit: do not deal treacherously.   Malachi 2:16

> They said, "Moses allowed one to write a certificate of divorce, and to dismiss her."
> Jesus said to them, "Because of your hardness of heart he wrote you this rule. But from the beginning of creation, 'male and female' He made them; 'On account of this a man shall leave his father and mother and shall cleave to his wife, and the two shall become one flesh – so then they are no longer two, but one flesh. Therefore what God has yoked together (unified), let no man divide."   Mark 10:4-9

In primitive cultures, breaking Covenant was viewed with abhorrence. The Covenant ceremony in Genesis 15 followed a common ritual which signified that "Should I break Covenant I will become as these lifeless carcasses – my life is forfeit." That the Source of Life would pledge this should astonish anyone, yet when He prophecies the breaking of Covenant in Hezekiah 11, the predicted setting is when Jesus is betrayed by Judas. And *God does die*. The original strength of Covenant, of which Marriage is a type, truly has the impact of "'Till death do we part." It is the Creator Himself Who provides the model, and identifies its seriousness – it is not an unimpassioned theoretical demand.

The point is not so much that there should be no divorce, but rather that this relationship requires such an awareness that one must be very careful before making a commitment of this encompassing a nature, whether in marriage- or in companion-Covenant. Considering how Covenant opens the door to the abuse of the relationship (look at the history of Israel throughout the Old Testament), this writer realized how very few people he would consider as candidates for such a commitment – no Covenant is to be entered into lightly. As the appalled disciples put it, "If such is the case of the man with his wife, it is better not to marry" [Matthew 19:10].

Of course, we live in a broken world and some have abused this truly *sacred* trust given to them by God and their spouses, as when a male or a female mercilessly seeks to control, to exert power for the sake of their own selfishness purposes – and there is no intent here to trivialize the tragedy of such misuse of God's arrangement. Yes, what we have now can be very distorted from the original design. Yes, it is necessary to be reserved in letting another have that kind of power over the core of our being.

That is why that time of discovery in courtship is so crucial, especially when attempting to do it hand-in-hand *with* the Lord. It is important to also remember that in spite of the mess we humans have made even in this key area of our purpose for being created ("the Image"), although the Lord has every reason to withdraw His plan, He has never done so. We talk a lot about how we should have faith in Him, yet here is a surprising area where

90

He has faith in *us* (with His intimate help of course – as the perfect Husband Himself would assist *His* Bride), and He still calls us to His vision of what we are to be.

Who Really is Mistrusted?

That brings us to the root problem in all of this. The rejection of "submission" actually stems from a far deeper problem than mere uneasiness about each other – it is a very ancient uncertainty which goes to the core of all people. In one form or another, the problem is a defiance which has been repeated ever since Genesis 3, where both Adam and Eve basically distrust Jehovah. They are suspicious even of *God*'s motives: Jehovah is holding back, depriving them of necessary and useful life-enhancing experiences, meanwhile requiring unreasonable demands – as Satan's temptation suggests:

> "For God knows that in the day you eat of it your eyes shall be opened, and you shall be as God, knowing good and evil." Genesis 3:5

"The man" and "the woman" are to reflect "the Image of God," yet they have significant skepticism about the "Original's" intentions and plans. When suspicion reigns within this key role of humankind, when the spiritual receiving equipment is filled with static, then it is no wonder that what they reflect everywhere else becomes muddled as well. From a nature that has been infected with the rebellion of sin, the ambivalence carries over into the pivotal relationship of marriage, in the joint expression of that "Image" through "male and female," especially to each other.

The Origin of "Submission"

St Paul indicates especially in Ephesians 5, that the "Original" which "the man" and "the woman" are to reflect is Jesus and His Bride. But looking closely at "the Head" (Jesus), we discover something surprising about "submission" – it is not a one-way street!

Consider the concept of Glory. Despite how we assume that it must mean majesty, power, control, we instead discover Jehovah defining it in terms of "goodness, Covenant relationship, mercy, grace, Steadfast Love, faithfulness, forgiveness, and justice" [Exodus 33:19; 34:6-7]. So also as we consider "headship," we naturally assume it means power, authority, and control, especially when it comes to the great Creator God – but servitude, subjection, and obedience also describe Him? One would think that the Almighty God would not be found dead doing anything so menial, so self-humbling!

Then again, perhaps He *was* found dead doing precisely that sort of thing:

> Who, in the days of His flesh, offered up pleadings and supplications, with forceful cries and tears in deep reverence, to Him Who had power to save Him out of death, and He was heard; though He was a Son, by the things which He suffered He learned obedience. Having been bought to completion, He became the Author of eternal salvation to all who obey Him   Hebrews 5:7-9

In fact, Jesus Himself declared that very same principle:

> even as the Son of Man came not to be served but to serve, and to give His Life as a Ransom for many.   Matthew 20:28; Mark 10:46

and again:

> For who is greater, he who reclines at the table, or he who serves? Is it not he who reclines at the table? I, however, am in your midst as He Who serves.
>
> Luke 22:27

Jesus submitted, yet in no way did it diminish His importance, His authority, His value, His personhood – or His equality with the Father. Our present human nature cannot conceive of "submission" without it also being a statement of diminishment. "Do nothing from selfishness or conceit, but in humility count others better than yourselves" [Philippians 2:3] and "For every one who exalts himself will be humbled, and he who humbles himself will be exalted" [Luke 14:11] are passages that can make us squirm.

Yet when such "submission" is truly within the nature of Jesus as the perfect "Image of the invisible God" [Colossians 1:15] then does not it challenge *all* who are created in that "Image" to reflect even *this* aspect, too?

> *Let this mind be in you which was also in Christ Jesus*, Who, though already in the nature of God, did not clutch at being equal with God, but neutralized Himself, taking the nature of a slave, having become the likeness of men. Being found in appearance as a man, He humbled Himself and became obedient even to death, even the death of the cross.
>
> Philippians 2:5-8

Unavoidably, the answer is Yes – the mirror cannot choose which characteristics it is pleased to show while hiding others. Either we are to reflect God – or we are left with trying to paste together a hodge-podge of little torn pieces all over the reflection – that is, if only God would stay still long enough.

Submission and Selfless Love

> ... man was created for a life of complete selfless love, whereby his actions would always be directed outward, toward God and neighbor, and never toward himself – whereby he would be the perfect image and likeness of God...
>
> Fr. John S. Romanides[31]

Do we really understand "submission"? Such "servitude" takes strength – it takes the Son of God Himself to submit:

> Jesus said to them, "My food is that I do the will of the One Who sent Me, and that I finish His work ... For I have come down out of heaven, not that I do My own will, but the will of the One Who sent Me."

And this is not just in regard to submission to His Father:

> If, therefore, I the LORD and the Teacher have then washed *your feet*, you also ought to wash one another's feet. For I have given you a pattern, that as I did to you, you also should do.　　　　　John 13:14-15

The same John who declares, "The Word became flesh and dwelt among us, and we beheld His Glory, the Glory as of the Only Begotten from the Father, full of grace and truth" [1:14], also later records Jesus saying, "If you had known Me, you would have known My Father also; and from now on you know Him and have seen Him. ... He who has seen Me has seen the Father" [14:7,9]. There with the washbasin at the feet of His disciples is the true and perfect "Image of God" at work! – and notice that Paul says that the man is to emulate Jesus as husband.

It could be argued that when God describes Himself as One Who has fed, clothed and otherwise cared for not only us but also all Creation [Psalm 145:15-16, Matthew 6:25-33], could such activity not easily describe a butler or some other servant? Jesus' servitude is indeed nothing novel, but rather in keeping with what Jehovah has constantly been doing for His creatures – and us – all along since His first act of creation. This path has been trod before by the Lord God Himself.

In fact, when Paul tells us that "the Head of Christ is God" [I Corinthians 11:3], is such submission within the God-head something that occurs as out-of-the-ordinary, only after and because of human sin; or is this simply what God does all the time, the way He operates internally anyway?

So when Paul instructs us to submit to each other, is he not merely telling us to truly be "the Image of God"? Therefore before we "jump on a bandwagon," whether it be anti-feminist or anti-submission, we need to consider against whom we are reacting. The human target (Paul) is very convenient, especially because whoever that human is will be flawed. But is not the real issue something that lies very deep in our human nature, that of the sin in us which detests this kind of reflecting *of the Lord*?

So apparently in Ephesians 5 Paul is not being *anti*-woman, but rather *pro*-"Image of God," which is why he appropriately prefaces his discussion of marriage relationships in terms of mutual "submission." And that is also the reason for the crucial perspective: he does not compare Jesus and His Bride, the Church, to human marriage, but rather the other way around – his eye is firmly fixed on "the Original."

Voluntary Submission

Notice, however, that Jesus is not forced into "taking orders" – His submission is voluntary , freely given – even heart-felt given: "Jesus said to them, 'My food is that I do the will of the One Who sent Me, and that I finish His work'" [John 4:34] and "then He said, 'Behold, O God, I have come to do Your will'" [Hebrews 10:9]. But it doesn't stop with the Father's will. He also voluntarily "takes on" the burdens of the humans whom He serves. He does not give theories or a "self-help" manual to those who struggle; He does not even "lend a hand" to ease the dead weight. No, He takes it *all* upon Himself:

that it might be fulfilled which was spoken through Isaiah the prophet, saying: "He Himself took our weaknesses and bore our incurable diseases."   Matthew 8:17

Who Himself bore our sins in His body on the tree, that, having died to sin, we might live for righteousness – from whose stripes you were healed.   I Peter 2:24

He endured hardship, rejection and disgrace. To buy His Bride from slavery, He Himself was sold for the price of a slave [Matthew 26:15, Exodus 21:32], and He purchased her by His own Blood, to "purify for Himself His own special People" [I Peter 1:18-19; Titus 2:14]. He washed her, not with mere water, but with the water from His side [John 19:34; I John 5:6,8] – the water connected to *the Word*. He still gives of Himself, Body and Soul – Body and Blood – to His Bride in Holy Communion. It had not been easy for Hosea to have loved Gomer so deeply, it has not been easy for Jehovah of Covenant to love His Bride so deeply. Yet for both Hosea and for Jehovah, it is what love is all about.   James Lindemann[32]

The character then of "submission" is something *given*, not imposed upon someone. That is a radical difference from the world around us which sees it as a result of force and conquest. In the hands of the Creator, its basis comes from deep within the heart in loving service to another, be it God or a fellow human. So mutual servitude is indeed the order of the day if we are to be true reflections of God:

Bear the burdens of one another, and so fulfill the law of Christ. ... For you were called to freedom, brethren; only do not use the freedom as a foothold for the flesh, but through Love serve one another. For the whole law is fulfilled in one word, in this: "You shall Love your neighbor as yourself."   Galatians 6:2; 5:13-14

There is a strange paradox here. On one hand, Jesus takes fully our burden in His submission to our needs. But there is also the counterpoint: we take His burden, His yoke, upon ourselves – we are to be "the Image of God"!

Come to Me, all you who toil to exhaustion and are burdened, and I will give you rest. Take My yoke upon you and disciple from Me, for I am humbly gentle and humble before God in heart, and you will find rest for your souls; for My yoke is suitable and useful, and My burden is easy to bear.   Matthew 11:28-30

The long and short of it all, is that Paul's comment about submitting to each other is not merely about two individuals who are uneasy about fully trusting each other, rather it is focused on a continuum of submission that begins with *God's* deliberate humbling of Himself. Then, since we are "the Image of God," this "submission" becomes reflected in all our relationships – with God, with others, and especially significantly with our spouse.

Submission, Not Capitulation

When Jehovah pronounces His discipline on Adam after the Fall, He prefaces it with "Because you have heeded the voice of your wife" [Genesis 3:17]. The man is to be the head of the family (discussed in chapter 10), but what is denounced here is that he has thrown aside this leadership. In other words, "mutual submission" cannot be used to undermine the responsibilities of being in "the Image of God." It is up to him to stand firm in his appointed office, heeding what St Paul would later identify:

If a man is overtaken in any trespass, you, the spiritual ones, restore him in a spirit of gentleness, considering yourself, lest you too be tempted.
                                                    Galatians 6:1

9. "The Weaker Vessel"

> Husbands, likewise, dwelling according to knowledge as with a weaker vessel, with the wife, rendering honor as joint-heirs of the grace of Life, so that your prayers are not hindered.
>
> I Peter 3:7

Defective

A comedian was once asked "How's your wife?" His reply was "Compared to what?" St Peter says that the woman is "a weaker vessel" – compared to what?

Just as we react to a word like "submit" or "helper" without understanding the environment in which they are used, the first problem with "a weaker vessel" comes because "weak" usually has a bad connotation, that of being defective or inadequate in some respect. Nobody likes the idea that he or she is "defective." In the rebellion of sin, where we are seeking not to reflect God but to usurp Him, admitting weakness is like "throwing in the towel" before the fight even begins.

It is important to identify that the "weakness" is not in reference to physical strength, or endurance, or mental prowess, or manipulative ability, or any of the other ways in which we try to play one-upmanship against each other. Rather St Peter is focused on the spiritual connection with God: "that your prayers are not hindered"; and therefore the framework for considering the idea of "weakness" is in regard to the task of reflecting "the Image of God."

On this basis then, we reluctantly acknowledge that we *all* are "weak." When compared to the Creator, we start out from the gates already woefully "inadequate," "defective," "weak." Some might say, "But if it weren't for sin, just imagine all that we would be capable of doing!" Various figures have been given which indicate that at any one time a human only utilizes a small fraction of what the brain is capable of doing. Of course, science *fiction* jumps in then with the idea that if we perked along at 100% or so, we could move things with our minds, understand vast complex mysteries, and so forth, and so on.

Perhaps. But that really is not so convincing. The problem with this attitude is that ultimately human nature wants to end up totally self-sufficient – we then would not be "weak," "defective," "inadequate." In the words of Satan's temptation, we would "become like God." Yet even the earthly Jesus, Who would have been running at full mental capacity, still insisted that His abilities were only "pass-through" powers – consider such statements as these:

> Do you not believe that I am in the Father and the Father is in Me? The words which I speak to you I do not speak from Myself; but the Father Who dwells in Me does His works.   John 14:10

> Jesus said to them, "Truly, truly, I say to you, the Son is able to do nothing from Himself, unless it is what He sees the Father doing; for whatever *He* does, these things the Son does likewise."   John 5:19

And if we were an untainted "Image of God," we also are at best,

> *His* handiwork, created in Christ Jesus for good works, which God prepared previously that we should walk in them.   Ephesians 2:10

Of course we are weak. A recent hailstorm which had baseball-sized hail for twenty minutes, or the drought that has caused farmers to harvest cornstalks since the ears were empty are stark demonstrations of our weakness to prevent them. We experience deep frustration at those in political power who no longer represent their constituents, but rather cater to whatever special interest groups have the deepest pockets for their re-election campaigns. No, we will never simply exert our will and make the universe or even this small slice of the universe conform to our wishes.

100

Designed Inadequacy

As we look at the opening quote for this chapter, the assumption is that the man comes from the position of power, while the woman come from the position of weakness. What we need to understand is that *both* come from the position of weakness.

Some of the "weakness" is by God's design. Humans were never created to be totally self-sufficient. Even in his most perfect state, the man is in need: the woman is created to be an essential "helper/savior" to him, and therefore she also is never meant to be independent in herself. Both together – not alone – are required to represent Creation's longed-for picture of "the Image of God." Even then, even together, "male and female" still could never begin to touch on all that Jehovah is.

It is fitting that this comes on the heels of the last topic, "submission." The bridge that connects that with this is the attitude of "humility" – of recognizing that, contrary to the desires of their rebellion, humans are not gods and never will be. Yes, in the interdependence into which they are created, they together have an extraordinary role (as "the Image of God"), an extraordinary honor (since Jehovah will not do many things unless by our hands), an extraordinary value (God became one of us to die and rescue us), among other such notable distinctions. Still, compared with the sheer greatness of God, humans will never be sufficient in and of themselves – they are "weak" by design.

In Heaven, too?

They will never outgrow the need for Jehovah. Although never spoken, there seems to be a vague idea that in heaven, with bodies and spirits recreated, now free from sin and its effects, humanity will finally "arrive" at that self-sufficiency that it craves. Other than for good friendship, will there be really any compelling need for Jesus or for the Holy Spirit? After all, a Savior will no longer be needed; no longer will the "Helper," the Holy Spirit, be needed to guide them through a no longer corrupted world, much less to assist the no longer broken human nature. No longer will "the man" and "the woman" be "defective," "inadequate," "weak" – or will they?

The reality is that there will never come a time when anyone will be self-sufficient, a time when Jesus and the Holy Spirit will not be needed. Such is the designed "weakness," that in order even to make it into the eternal Kingdom, then must *"the God of peace Himself* sanctify you wholly; and may the whole of you, the Spirit and the Soul and the Body, be kept blameless in the coming of our Lord Jesus Christ. Faithful is He Who calls you, *and He will do it"* [I Thessalonians 5:23-24]. Even in heaven, if we ever were to step outside of our Lord (which will not happen), we would be lost. There will never come a time when we will not need the Holy Spirit, His guidance and wisdom. It is just that we will finally actually *listen* to Him and cooperate with Him – and be the partner with our Bridegroom that we were created to be – now in that new Creation.

The designed inadequacy will simply and intentionally not be resolved – and the reflection of "the Image" will always require both the masculine and the feminine traits.

The Weakness of Sin

Being told that we will always be "weak" and "inadequate" does not make our human nature happy, which brings us to a second aspect of being "weak," which comes from the rebellion of sin. Because of this disconnection from God, there is a deterioration in regard to all that we are in Body, Soul and Spirit. It is such a catastrophic deterioration that even the universe experiences it ("entropy"), as it struggles from the curse of Genesis 3:17, and revolts against the rebel man (v 18). The ultimate "weakness," of course, is death, where we are in absolute helplessness – as demonstrated by the fact that, except for One, no human has been able to get up and return to life by his own wish.

In the physical, the Bible uses "weakness" to indicate sickness [for example, Mathew 25:39ff; Luke 10:9; Acts 5:15-16]; physical limitations ("The spirit indeed is willing, but the flesh is weak" [Matthew 26:41]); and feebleness ("... but his bodily presence is weak, and his speech contemptible" [II Corinthians 10:10, also I Corinthians 2:3]). There can be a physical malaise when healthy care is not taken in regard to *spiritual* matters ("he who eats and drinks in an unworthy manner eats and drinks discipline on himself, not discerning the Lord's Body. For *this* reason many are weak and sick among you, and many sleep" [I Corinthians 11:29-30]).

One can be spiritually weak (often founded upon a lack of knowledge or understanding) which brings about a weakness in the conscience [I Corinthians 8:7-10, I Thessalonians 5:14]. One may then turn to "the weak and beggarly elements, to which you desire again to be in bondage" [Galatians 4:9], which makes a person a "slave of uncleanness, and of lawlessness leading to more lawlessness" [Romans 6:19]. Even the Law, "the former commandment" is described as "weak and unprofitable" [Hebrews 7:18].

The Third Weakness

So there are two types of "weakness": one by design; one from the distortion of sin. However, what really makes the subject go wild is a third "weakness," where it can also be God's badge of honor – consider:

But the foolish things of the *cosmos* God chose in order that He might shame the wise, and the weak things of the *cosmos* God chose in order that He might shame the strong. I Corinthians 1:27

He said to me, "My grace is sufficient for you, for indeed power is perfected in weakness." Most gladly therefore will I rather boast in my weaknesses, that the power of Christ may dwell upon me. Therefore I am pleased in weaknesses, in insults, in dire need, in persecutions, in distresses, for Christ's sake; for when I am weak, then I am strong. II Corinthians 12:9,10

But, much more, the members of the body which seem to be weaker are necessary; those of the body which we think to be less honorable, around these we wrap more abundant honor; and our unpresentable parts have more abundant modesty, while our presentable parts have no such need. But God blended the body together, having given that which is inferior the greater honor. I Corinthians 12:22-24

Before we look with disdain upon "weakness," we are called to realize that some of God's best work occurs in "weakness": "For though He was crucified in weakness, yet He lives by the power of God. For we also are weak in Him, but we shall live with Him by the power of God toward you" [II Corinthians 13:4]. It is that ultimate weakness called "death" in which Jehovah saved the world, and in the above second quote, Paul declares that he treasures weakness because that is where God's power can be fully expressed.

The Earthen Vessel

We have spent some time on the "weaker" part of Peter's phrase "the weaker vessel," but what is the concept behind "vessel"? As a side note, the word is not "sex"(gender) as the RSV has it, but rather "vessel": the focus is on something greater than body features and role in procreation. A "vessel" can mean an instrument, as for instance someone who is chosen for a special task, which fits very well the human task of reflecting God. But perhaps the first thought is that of a container. If so, then what is it holding?

But we have this treasure in earthen vessels, so that the superiority of the power may be of God and not from us.   II Corinthians 4:7

What then would be that "treasure in earthen 'vessels'"? In the previous verse, St Paul states, "For it is God Who said, 'Out of darkness light shall shine,' Who has shone in our hearts to illuminate the knowledge of the Glory of God in the face of Jesus Christ." The role of this "Glory" is identified six verses earlier, "But we all, with unveiled face, beholding the Glory of the Lord as in a mirror, are being transformed into the same Image from Glory to Glory, exactly as from the Lord the Spirit" [3:18]. We find ourselves again pivoting around "the Image of God" theme. The "weak," "helpless," "inadequate" – these earthen vessels – have an extraordinary privilege of "containing" the "the Image of God," particularly "the Glory of God in the face of Jesus Christ." Both "male and female" are equally necessary in this, just as, if a mirror is to "contain" an image, it requires both the glass and the silvering.

In fact, although she is indeed the creation second to man, the woman is by no means of incidental importance, as Paul also identifies:

For man is not from woman, but woman from man. Nor was man created on account of the woman, but woman on account of the man. … Nevertheless, neither is man independent of woman, nor woman independent of man, in the Lord. For as woman is from man, even so man also comes through woman; and all things are from God.
                    I Corinthians 11:8-12

As emphasized here and in I Timothy 2:13 "For Adam was formed first, then Eve," we cannot get away from the fact that Eve is created to respond to Adam's need, a need far greater than merely for procreation, a need regarding his central identity of carrying "the Image of God" before all Creation. The paradox of the human in being the weak earthen vessel which holds the Glory and the Image of God is evident here. Although she is called "the weaker vessel," she is also designed to be *God's* "helper/savior" for the man, the same paradox of simultaneously being "defective" and having God's power. In a totally virgin birth – without any "help" from man – "God sent forth His Son, born of a woman" [Galatians 4:4]. In the "weakness" of the woman is found God's great saving activity.

The Fall of the Earthen Vessel

But as discussed previously, it is in her function as "helper" that her vulnerability lies. "Adam was not deceived, but the woman being deceived, entered into transgression" [I Timothy 2:14] – it is interesting how this relates to the previously quoted definition of "Feminist Ethics," where the masculine "autonomy, intellect, will … rule, rights, … and impartiality" are "overrated," while "emotion, … trust, … joy, peace, and life," are "underrated."

Eve is deceived into thinking that detaching her basic identity from the will of God is incidental in favor of sin's "good intentions," as well as of rebellion's "benefits" not just to herself, but also to her family. Again, the "weakness" has little to do with strength of muscle, intelligence, wisdom, cunning, or the like; it is at root a *spiritual* vulnerability – it has to do with turning away from Jehovah, not just toward the fantasized "benefits."

By comparison to that, the man is not deceived – no, he quite knowingly jumps into rebellion with both feet. His "weakness" is that he does not want to be merely the middle man. She may think she is "helping" and therefore is deceived, but he wants to simply shuck off responsibility toward his Creator. He is not so much taken by all the perks to which the woman is attracted, but rather like Satan he is more interested in simply usurping God's place. She may be susceptible to deception, but in discarding the will of God, the man deliberately does what is foolish and destructive to everything, even to himself. She is called "the weaker vessel," but when it comes to man's "strength," it is more fitting that he hang his head in shame.

The "Stronger" Vessel

How ironic it is, pondering how Adam "listened to the voice of [his] wife and ate of the tree" [Genesis 3:17], along with the fall of Samson [Judges 16], David [II Samuel 11:1-5], Solomon [I Kings 11:1-10] and others, that the man is assumed to be the "stronger" vessel.

Yet he can be, he can indeed be the one who leads humanity into the real "Strength" that "the Image of God" can have:

> Jehovah is my Strength and Song – He has become Salvation to me; He is my God, I will praise Him; my father's God, I will exalt Him.
>
> Exodus 15:2

> Jehovah, my Strength, I love You. Jehovah is my Rock, my Fortress, my Deliverer; my God, my High Ground, in Whom I take Refuge; My Shield and the Horn of my Salvation, my Stronghold. Psalm 18:1-2

> But those who wait on Jehovah shall grow in strength; they shall mount up with wings as eagles, they shall run and not be weary, they shall walk and not be faint.
>
> Isaiah 40:31

The reason why "the man" and "the woman" exist is so that they will be God's reflection in Creation, and that task revolves around being the expression of "the Glory of God" with all the attributes which we identified previously. Therefore the definition of man's "strength" must be based on *this* reason for his existence – any attempt based on other criteria, usually on a self-centered one, is doomed to miss entirely how "strength" fits into this connection with God. It will miss how "weakness" is actually an essential piece in "strength," as the man in humility "submits" to his "need" for a "helper" – and for "the Helper."

As the one created in response to the man's need, the woman is to take her cue from the man, to find her strength in *God's* strength as reflected in the man. Although she is responsible for her own actions, yet when the man removes a necessary supporting structure for his "helper" – the spiritual dependence on his Creator - he only magnifies the woman's weakness. In essence, Paul in the quote at the beginning of this chapter is telling the man to put that support back, the support that she is to depend on.

It is best we dispense with the competitiveness that we are so eager to use to justify ourselves, and instead simply confess our common "weaknesses" in God's design (where we *need* each other), in the weakness that has resulted through the Fall into rebellion, and in the weakness that requires us to discover our strength in "the Helper," Who has not just created us but also has saved us.

When "male and female" are properly aligned to God's will, where both are mindful of both the man's and the woman's vulnerabilities, where both accept the mutual dependency on and strength from each other, where both take seriously being in God's will as they carry out their common task of being His "Image," where they depend on His strength in their "weakness" – then comes the effect that Peter describes, "being heirs together of the grace of life, that your prayers may not be hindered." Within the proper relationship between Jehovah, the man and the woman, all kinds of spiritual and other doors open up in our lives.

10. Headship

But I wish you to perceive that the Head of every man is Christ, the head of a woman is man, and the Head of Christ is God.

I Corinthians 11:3

A Characteristic of "The Image of God"

Especially in Ephesians 5 when St Paul instructs wives to submit "to your own husbands as to the Lord; for the husband is head of the wife, as also Christ is Head of the Church; and He is the Savior of the Body" [vv 22-23], often the reaction is swift and vehement: "No one will be boss of *me*!"

But as already mentioned in chapter 8, "headship" is the counterpoint of "submission," and as the I Corinthians quote above identifies, both begin internally within the Godhead. These attitudes are actually but a characteristic of Jehovah, reflected by Paul's Ephesians instruction beginning with *mutual* submission [v 21], thereby making visible Jesus submitting to His Father and His becoming Servant to His Church, as well as the Father serving the needs of Creation. How odd it is to think of *God* being humble, much less *that* humble!

Although it just simply does not happen, what if God the Son refused to submit to God the Father, or the Holy Spirit to God the Son? Even a "benevolent" dictator, if he does not get the cooperation he expects, will fall back to his army when he feels it is required, but here, "sending in the army" is ludicrous. The point is: "it just simply does not happen" – why? What is there about that internal relationship where a challenge against "headship" just does not occur?

It is indeed very unusual for our world: the qualities of "headship" and of "submission" are founded not upon force and conquest, but upon deep love, humility and self-giving – from the Creator no less!

The commission, therefore, of being "the Image of God" certainly has a way of upsetting our comfortable private lives and egos! As Jesus freely submits to His Father, as the Church freely submits to her Lord, so the wife is to freely submit to her husband. On the other hand, the husband's headship only begins as he freely submits to *his* Head, Jesus [I Corinthians 11:3]. He is to reflect the "Image" of his Lord, Who in turn has submitted to and reflects *His* Head: "If you had known Me, you would have known My Father also; and from now on you know Him and have seen Him. ... He who has seen Me has seen the Father" [John 14:7,9] – or to paraphrase for the husband, "If you have known me, you would also have known my Jesus, and from now on, you know Him and have seen Him ... He who has seen me has seen Jesus."

Ultimately, one's "headship" can be understood only as a "pass-through" power, where each is accountable to represent his/her own Head/head. If "the Image of God" is being reflected, then which way one faces is key here: is the "Head/head" filling the picture, or is one's back turned in order to focus on whether others are "toeing the line"? "The Image" is no photograph – the Object being reflected has to be "real time" – constant, living and present tense.

"Follow Me"

How then should we think of "headship"? Perhaps a look at how Napoleon treated his troops can give us an idea:

Abbott, the historian, tells us that one characteristic of Napoleon was that he never commanded any soldier in his ranks to go where he

110

himself was not willing to lead him. On one occasion, he ordered his army to cross a river; but seeing them hesitate to obey, the emperor spurred forward his horse crying: "Soldier, follow your general!" He was first to plunge into the river and first to reach the other side. Needless to say, his army to a man followed him cheering as with one voice their bold leader.

Unknown

How then might the headship of the husband be accomplished in his family? Well, *his* Head put it succinctly: "come, follow Me" [Matthew 19:21[33]]. As Jesus reflects His Head, we are shown "the illumination of the Gospel of the Glory of Christ, Who is the image of God, ... to illuminate the knowledge of the Glory of God in the face of Jesus Christ" [II Corinthians 4:4,6]: "we have seen His Glory, the Glory as of the Only Begotten of the Father, full of grace and truth" [John 1:14].

We are back again with the concept of "Glory." Although it does include many things, John's quote reminds us how Jehovah defined it in Exodus 33 and 34, which reveals a window into His very nature: His goodness, Covenant relationship, grace, mercy, Steadfast Love, faithfulness, forgiveness, and justice. These are important safeguards against the abuses into which people can so easily fall.

According to Paul, as the man reflects his Head, he is to be "the Image and Glory of God" [I Corinthians 11:7]. The aim of his headship is to orient male and female both (since Paul does not here specify a gender) to behold "the Glory of the Lord as in a mirror, are being transformed into the same Image from Glory to Glory, exactly as from the Lord the Spirit." [II Corinthians 3:18].

The qualities of God's Glory are not easy to express in one's life, which is why the man's relationship to his Head cannot be a photograph but a mirror – this relationship has to be alive, growing; the "Image" has to be made clearer and clearer.

As the husband enters into the field of God's Glory, he is the pathfinder, the scout, the trail-breaker, the leader who explores deep into the qualities of God, with all the challenges that come in this world. He shows his family the way – not to be "successful," but rather to be God's People in their lives, modeling his life after his Head's, that his family may model their lives after his – and that he may discover, as Jesus leads him and his family,

> that the God of our Lord Jesus Christ, the Father of Glory, may give to you the spirit of wisdom and revelation in the knowledge of Him, the eyes of your heart being enlightened, that you may perceive what is the hope of His calling, what are the riches of the Glory of His inheritance in the saints. Ephesians 1:17-18

Humility

When we are told to be humble before the Lord, are we left to generate it on our own? Of course not; we are to reflect what He is, and as discussed earlier this is not something outside of the "Image." When Jesus washes the feet of His disciples, this is not merely an episode as an object lesson but is a quality which God Himself has.

St Paul tells the Philippians to "in humility esteem one another as above themselves" [2:3 – "above" can mean better or more important] – where does this idea come from? From the cross. Jesus has put us above Himself; He has made us more important than Himself – He has counted Himself expendable on our behalf, He has put our life above His own. We often think of humility as directed toward a superior – for example, God the Father – but Jesus counts humanity as more important than Himself.

Could humility be a characteristic of the Creator? He feeds and clothes His creation – birds, animals, plants, humans [Matthew 5:26-34] – even counting the hairs of the head [Matthew 10:29-31]. He nurses Israel along even though it is a most rebellious child, patiently dealing with tantrum after tantrum., rejection after rejection, continually forgiving, continually calling them back to Himself. Ultimately He will die for them – all for their benefit, not His own.

Internally within the Godhead as well, when the Father sends His only Son, Who submits to this mission, this humility occurs *before* Jesus comes into the flesh. When Jesus says, "the Father is greater than I" [John 14:28], we are quick to say that this is only as the earth-bound Jesus ("in His humility" [Ephesians 2:8]) speaks, but is this really so? Or is this the humility which "counts another as more important than oneself" – a humility which the Godhead has within its Persons from eternity? After all, Jesus has no need to prove Himself nor assert His equality within the Godhead. There is only the humility in which the three Persons not only act as One, but *are* One.

So when Paul writes "Husbands, love your wives, just as Christ also loved the Church and gave Himself up for her" [Ephesians 5:25], and "Wives, submit to your own husbands as to the Lord' [v 22], this is the affirmation that they are indeed to be "the Image of God" in the *totality* of the reflection. This is why Paul can so fearlessly call upon us all to be "subject to one another *out of reverence for Christ*" [Ephesians 5:21] and therefore the wife is enabled to reflect *her* head, as he reflects *his* Head Jesus, Who reflects His Head.

But is Paul not describing a relationship of Love here? It seems that humility and Love are very interrelated.

Of course, due to our fallen human nature, the reflection is never as clear as it was designed to be. Within the history of families, men have given sometimes very unfortunate portrayals (either too harsh or too soft) of Jesus, and therefore of the Father. However, this does not thereby give permission to simply discard the task and dismiss the human, neither by the man, nor by the woman, nor by God. The Master Craftsman has never retracted His design – it still has validity even in our fallen world of today. The defects are to be patched by love and forgiveness by both God and human – the same as our Head and His Head have done for all of us, despite *our* failings.

The reality for us all is as Paul declares: "for all have sinned and fall short of the *Glory* of God" [Romans 3:23]. Why are the ones entrusted with such an awesome honor also such fallible creatures? Truly, some do not care about what their position as head of the family means, but many do take seriously this high calling and are frustrated that they can be so fumbling at something so important. After all, when the wife and the children's pivotal experience of Jehovah (in the reflection of "the Image") is through the chain of Headship, through their husband and father, this is far from trivial.

To Know the Love

> that Christ may dwell through faith in your hearts; that you, being rooted and founded in Love, may a full capacity to comprehend with all the saints what is the width, length, depth and height, and to know with transcending knowledge the Love of Christ; that you may be filled with all the fullness of God.   Ephesians 3:17-19

The Hebrew word for "know" is a very comprehensive word, but there are three important meanings to consider (as defined by the Online Bible Hebrew Lexicon):

> 1a1b) to perceive
> 1a1d) to discriminate, distinguish
> 1a1e) to know by experience[34]

When Satan advances his temptation, he promises particularly the "to know by experience" meaning in that "you will be like God, knowing good and evil" [Genesis 3:6], and, yes, the "temptees" get first-hand knowledge of

114

good and evil. Unfortunately, they also lose the "to perceive" knowledge, particularly in regard to God. No longer can they see Jehovah for what He is. No longer will the husband clearly reflect the compassionate Ruler in His wise and loving management of Creation, nor represent the true picture of the Glory of God. No longer will the wife accurately demonstrate the basic knowledge about *God's* Love, care, forgiveness, mercy and the rest. No longer will the child take this "knowledge by experience" from both of these "Images of God," especially from the father (often the concept of God is based upon one's experience of one's father), not have an adequate perception of the "the Original," his/her heavenly Father.

To reverse this, as the pacesetter of the family, the father must humbly and deliberately follow his Head, Who is described in Word and Sacrament, and revealed through His Church. Through the Holy Spirit's power, he gets "to know" Jehovah from "the Diary of His Heart and Mind" (the Bible), listening to His thoughts and seeing His actions, and through fellow humans (especially his wife who is God's helper/savior) he increasingly is brought face-to-face with "God's love which has been poured into our hearts through the Holy Spirit Who has been given to us" [Romans 5:5]. By these experiences he comes "to know with transcending knowledge the Love of Christ." Now he is equipped to more clearly reflect Jesus.

Still, this is not enough – as one infected by sin, the father cannot by himself adequately reflect his Head. Despite how good a glimpse the father may give a child (or Creation) as to what the Lord is like, still he and his wife will always have incompletes, inconsistencies, inaccuracies and other shortcomings in what they reflect. This requires a sort of *binocular* vision: although one eye is on the practical concrete demonstration of these humans, another eye must also be kept on "the Original" Jesus. The real world experience from husband and wife along with the God's own account of His thoughts and actions creates a 3D view of God, with depth beyond what may seem to some as only a 2-Dimensional appearance in the Bible.

In this binocular view will also be the balance: some impressions from the parents will be built on, and some will have to be overcome. In some cases we will delight in and cherish the portrayal by the parents, and in others we yearn for "the Original's" difference. The child is better equipped to glimpse the greater God Who stands behind the reflections, not only for his own understandings, but also for the world and for all Creation to see.

Real-Life Forgiveness

Of course, the task is daunting. The man as well as the woman will fail in their portrayal of "the Original" – it is a "given," since we are infected with the rebellion which has spiritually-genetically infected all humanity.

Yet even the failures are useful. In the father's admission that heis not a perfect representation of his Head, there is the opportunity for the family together to look to Jesus and find that perfection. But he must also understand that he is not now outside of God's plan – neither has he been released from the responsibility nor is he to be rejected! He has opened the door, so to speak, through what he has been able to reflect, and then must encourage his family on to greater awareness of what Jesus has for them, which is far greater than what he is able to portray; he is then to lead them to see the Ideal Head that stands above him.

As well, he has a wonderful opportunity to demonstrate to his family what the death and resurrection of Jesus is all about. There is hope for himself, and therefore for each member of his family, because he and they are surrounded by an astonishing forgiveness made available by his Head. Here is a necessary and valuable way by which the family discovers that Jesus is more than some great Leader or Teacher – He is also Savior and

116

Redeemer. How else will they get to "see" Him in *all* His Glory except that He comes into their family circle with the forgiveness which He has so dearly won for them!

The father then has the opportunity to show how he also lives in forgiveness, reflecting to his family the value of Paul's principle: "one thing I do, forgetting what is behind and straining forward to what is ahead" [Philippians 3:13 – written by the man who had once been "as to zeal a persecutor of the Church" v 6; also Acts 26:10] – There is now a wonderful freedom for life that gives him and his family release from the past!

Human Nature's Rebellion

When *our* human nature retorts to *Jehovah*, "I am *not* going to let *You* boss *me* around and tell *me* what I can do!", it is too easy to have the same reaction to His "Image" in someone else. This can happen within a marriage setting, but also in how one reacts to a speed limit, a seatbelt law, a warning about danger, a "Do not walk on the grass" sign, a "do not eat the fruit of a certain tree" command [Genesis 2:16-18], or any of hundreds of other situations where we refuse to have *anybody* tell *us* what we should do.

As discussed previously, "trust" has a curious fickleness in which one pledges his or her life to the other, then, in essence, turns and says, "but I really do not trust you with my life; I do not believe you really care about my welfare; I alone know what is best for *me*."

Adding to this is the unpleasant realization that we are weak – deliberately designed so. Neither the man nor the woman is self-sufficient, but deliberately designed to be a two-part "Image": "male and female He created them." However, our human nature does not want to be just "the Image of God" – it wants to be God, and it annoys our nature to have to admit this, much less to place ourselves into submission to *anyone* else.

This is no minor battle with God's will, whether for the man in reflecting his Head, or for the woman in reflecting her head, and is not easily fought. Although the Holy Spirit is an essential element in the whole "headship" and "submission" transaction ("no one can say that Jesus is Lord except by the Holy Spirit" [I Corinthians 12:3]), the warning we have is that we can also thwart "the Image" that we mirror – we can "quench the Spirit"[I Thessalonians 5:19], "grieve the Holy Spirit of God" [Ephesians 4:30], and "resist the Holy Spirit" [Acts 7:51].

This is important if we are to reflect Jehovah. As we look at Jesus' submission, we must also pay attention to the standard raised in Philippians 2: "Let this mind be in you which was also in Christ Jesus, … He humbled Himself and became obedient to the point of death, even the death of the cross" [vv 5,8]. Will "humility" – especially before Jehovah – be an element that characterizes the relationship between "male and female"?

Power or Weakness?

A tension is evident where the husband is to be the leader. Although Napoleon led his troops, he still also directed them and had final say about their course of action. As we have seen many times in war, sometimes the person in that position can be a fool.

So there are some reasonable fears in regard to trusting another person with one's self and future. There is risk and the danger of abuse. When marriage becomes a "power" relationship, then Lord Acton's warning speaks of a real concern: "Power tends to corrupt and absolute power corrupts absolutely." Indeed, some take the idea of "headship" to give permission for the abuse of power.

However, our various Bible texts remind us that this is not to be a power relationship. As mentioned, *humility* surrounds this subject – humility

118

both of the man and of the woman. The husband's authority does not lie within himself, being "the Image of God" is only a "pass-through" power. He is to reflect particularly Jesus in His Glory as previously defined, *and is also accountable to Him.*

The prophet Hosea provides a remarkable example of humility, although having power, he instead earnestly desired a relationship built upon Steadfast Love. Gomer, his wife, had returned to her unfaithful ways, even while Hosea had been supporting her (while she had a live-in lover). She still accumulated such debt that she finally was to be sold into slavery. When the prophet discovered this, he bought her – she was twice his, by marriage and now by ownership:

> Yet, despite all that she had done to abuse him, to reject him, and to cause him pain, Hosea was not interested in a power relationship – of such was *not* the love he still felt for her. Instead he prescribed a period of mutual celibacy, a sort of sexual detoxification to break the cycle of her addiction [3:3-4]. The ultimate goal in the text read at the beginning was when "it shall be, in that day,... that you will call Me 'My Husband' and no longer call Me 'My Master'" [2:16; 3:5]. Since Hosea's relationship to Gomer paralleled Jehovah's relationship with Israel, both the prophet and God's intent was to patiently nurture the smoldering ember of love into its full fire.   James Lindemann[35]

This means that a husband must be very careful to accurately reflect *his* Head, mirroring what is to be found in his Lord, where it is *Steadfast Love* which provides the pivot, not "the desire to control." This is why the Christian background, especially of the husband, is not incidental. Unless he knows his place with Jesus and His grace and mercy, he will not have the full depth of understanding as to what his role is to be with his wife.

And since the wife's head is her husband, as he says in essence, "follow me!", he can give her the solid platform to also *reflect his humility,* just as he reflects the humility of Jesus, *his* Head – both of which are intentional attitudes.

When "the Image" Is Not There

When everyone is doing their task properly, then the wife will be the image of her head, who should be the reflection of his Head. But if he is derelict in this "reflection," does this constitute permission to throw such humbleness, subjection and the rest out the window?

Ultimately, according to Genesis 1:26, the woman is just as involved in the task of being "the Image of God" as the man. Paul insists in Ephesians 5 that her model is the Church, to whom our Lord said, "If, therefore, I the Lord and the Teacher have then washed your feet, you also ought to wash one another's feet. For I have given you a pattern, that as I did to you, you also should do." [John 13:14-15].

When the husband is disconnected from his role as head, this is an area where eternity wrestles with the temporal. St Peter puts it this way:

> Likewise wives, submitting to your own husbands, so that even if any disobey the Word, that through the behavior of their wives they may be won without a word, having witnessed your spotless behavior in reverence. ... but let it be the hidden person of the heart with the incorruptible gentle and quiet spirit, which in God's sight is very precious.   I Peter 3:1-2,4

The struggle is in regard to our values: is the cost of humility, of putting second our own here-and-now unmet dreams and ideals, worth the risk of submitting in order to truly reflect "the Image"? In fact, is it worthwhile if it can mean that the spouse may be led to the Lord? Does an eternal goal outweigh our private ambitions? In a culture in which one is defined by power – income power, manipulation power, prestige power, advancement power – what does it mean to reflect "the Image of God," especially in

120

reference to *His* humility? What values are to reflect Jesus and His Bride, the Church? Do we stand against, or merely be swept along with modern society's value system?

Abuse of Position

However, there is a problem that stems from Peter's "likewise" (above), which refers back three verses [2:23]: "When [Jesus] was reviled, He did not revile in return; when He suffered, He did not threaten; but He trusted in Him Who judges justly." This now gets sticky. Truly, no one will be perfect in one's role and task in marriage – neither the husband nor the wife. But what about an abusive relationship? How far is humility and submitting to headship to go?

Actually, since either spouse can be abusive, this not only covers the submission of the wife to an abusive husband as head, it can also deal with the husband's submission to his Head, Jesus, in the midst of being reviled by and suffering from an abusive wife. How far are we to be humble, how far do we go in putting aside our ambitions, and even comfort, for the sake of eternity? Ideally, we should reflect Jesus, even if it "costs" us: "focusing on the Author and Perfecter of our faith, Jesus, Who for the joy set before Him endured the Cross, despising the shame, and has sat down at the right hand of the throne of God" [Hebrews 12:2].

Sometimes abuse may not be of a violent nature. In the story told earlier,[36] in regard to Samuel Clemens (Mark Twain) and his wife Livy (Olivia), his ridicule of Christianity finally overwhelmed her faith, until there was nothing left for the time when she needed it.

What is especially awkward in Peter's statement above is "so that *some* ... may be won": there is no guarantee of an outcome. Even with Jesus, a large group of people for whom He died have reviled Him to their deaths.

Peter, who has watched fellow Christians suffer and die for their faith, is not treating the wife's humility and submission callously. He does understand the extreme cost. But he also understands what the stakes are, even when such humility will cost his own life on an upside-down cross.

He makes his comments not as if the woman's submission to her husband is in isolation, but rather in view of how it occurs within first humbly submitting *to her Lord*. In an abusive relationship, one tends to be overwhelmed by the abusive partner's opinions. Unlike what happened to Livy, one must constantly reaffirm the value and worth that her Savior has placed on her in order to give balance to what she encounters. This is what Hebrews 12 (above) means by "Who for the joy set before Him" – the long-range, eternal meaning to her life is established by Jesus' opinion, value and action for her, which no one else can take away from her.

We are social creatures, whether female or male, despite how many sources (our own human nature included) attempt to isolate us. It was no accident when Jehovah in the Old Testament formed the People of God, and Jesus in the New gathered around Himself the Church. The person under abuse strongly needs support, not for a husband (or wife) bashing orgy, nor for a "pity party," but rather for an environment where she (or he) is affirmed in the Lord's powerful love for her (and him), as well as reminded of the capabilities, abilities, strengths and hope which she (and he) has and which surround her (and him). As those who have been in concentration, prisoner of war and death camps (for example, Corrie ten Boom's experience in *The Hiding Place*) have demonstrated, Jesus can still be found even in the worst of conditions, particularly when fellow believers uphold each other.

Divorce

However, it is hard to stand against intense abuse, and humanly speaking it is hard to hold on. Too often evil can be relentless. There are times when Paul tells his readers to *flee* certain types of evil [I Corinthians 6:18; 10:14; I Timothy 6:11; II Timothy 2:22]. In the Mark Twain-Livy example above, do we tell Livy she should stay, where she did experience the continual erosion of her faith; or do we tell her to leave him, while reminded that "Jehovah God of Israel ... hates divorce, for it covers one's garment with violence" [Malachi 2:16]? Where is the Solomon who can predict the correct course of action?

Truly we should consult the Lord, and yet even that is hard because there is so much shame involved (just like Adam and Eve hiding after the Fall). It is not easy to admit when we discover how weak, even in faith, that we are. Sometimes in pure weariness we find we must take ourselves out of the battle.

It must be noted that divorce is to be the direst of last resort, because it does "cover one's garment with violence" [Malachi 2:16], as many who have experienced divorce will affirm. Paul strongly encourages that the couple stay together, yet this will not always be the case. There may be a time when husband and wife must part ways:

> To the rest, I say – not the Lord –, that if any brother has an unbelieving wife, and she consents to dwell with him, he should not leave her. If any woman has an unbelieving husband, and he consents to dwell with her, she should not leave him. For the unbelieving husband is sanctified in the wife, and the unbelieving wife is sanctified in the husband, else your children are unclean but now they are holy. But if the unbeliever separates oneself, let it be so; the brother or sister is not bound in such cases. For God has called us in peace. However, wife, how do you know whether you will save your husband; or, husband, how do you know whether you will save your wife? I Corinthians 7:12-16

The issue is vastly larger than "what pleases *me*" or "what makes *me* happy," or the lack thereof, which is often the gauge for marriage and divorce in our culture. As "the Image of God," representing His self-giving Love (even for His enemies [Romans 5:6-10]), Paul calls us to consider what Love truly wants for the other person. Ultimately, our task is not our own gratification – the stated purpose for the existence of humanity is to make the Creator visible and that is the challenge Paul lays before us.

This may also answer the puzzle of Paul's comment "else your children are unclean but now they are holy." The children would be made "unclean" by divorce? They would be made "holy" by the parents remaining together? Yet then he continues in the next verse that if the unbeliever wants to separate, then it should be allowed – so what does this do to his argument about the children? Will they not then become "unclean"?

To understand this in "the Image of God" context, the child is better equipped to discover his contribution within the "Image" when he experiences the reflection by *both* parents, even when one parent is not conscious of what he is doing. The Greek word for "unclean" can mean "not pure," often because it is mixed with something other than what is godly. Could it mean here not a mixture of "godly" and "ungodly" but rather the *absence* of something, so that in that way the "purity" is defective? This interpretation would give substance to the modern recommendation for single parents to have someone of the opposite sex also involved in the life of their children in order to help give them a balanced view of genders and of humanity.

As we consider this very difficult subject, truly there are times when we have dug ourselves into such a deep hole, because of bad judgment, foolishness, or ignorance, that the only way out is through repentance and forgiveness, and that Baptism's "new birth" allows for a new beginning.

This is not for an easy way out, but rather in the misery of our sinful condition, we must humbly confess that we need a Savior.

The Joy Set Before Us

Obviously, the goal is the proper headship order in which "the Image of God" is visibly demonstrated. When it is not, or is not comfortable, our nature often casually "tips the hat" to the concept, but then is very quick to jump toward easier, more convenient and less spiritually costly solutions. However, if we are to seek God's will, then humility, submission, and values must be faced: first, humility and submission to the Lord; then humility and submission to each other; and third, humility before the eternal values that must be contrasted with the earthly values. God never said it would be pleasant to be His person in this world, just as it was by no means pleasant for Jesus to totally submit to the will of His Father, but He does indicate that there will be joy in it in the end.

11. The Helper's Participation

Let a woman learn in "silence" with all submission. I do not allow a woman to teach or to have authority over a man, but to be in "silence."

I Timothy 2:11-12

Awkward

Is Paul saying that women, like children, are "to be seen and not heard"? Care must be exercised not to isolate a passage from the greater context and balance that the Bible may have on any subject, and this one in particular. As well, what concept did the original language, Greek, have in regard to the word "silence"? And finally, one must also keep in mind that human nature is often offended by some of the things God says to us.

Although that may sound ominous, it is not a forewarning that this must be a negative and unpleasant topic, although it may be a hard one. For the moment, consider John 6 as Jesus declares that "unless you eat the Flesh of the Son of Man and drink His Blood, you have no Life in you" [v 53], which results in "Therefore many of His disciples, having heard this, said, 'This saying is hard – who is able to understand it?' ... From that time many from His disciples turned back and walked no more with Him" [vv 60, 66].

In reality, Jesus is declaring comforting news that will take tangible shape later in Holy Communion: there is forgiveness, life, and a deep personal relationship to be had from this "Bread from Heaven" (Jesus). Yet the people do not want to hear of it – the human nature, which is so anti-God, ends up rejecting even what is good. So it is important then to look carefully at what it is to which we are reacting and why. Our offense at God's Word may actually not be as "honorably" and even "self-righteously" motivated as we think.

Silence!

Looking at the I Timothy 2 passage, what is the swing of Paul's argument previous to the given verses? He has just counseled that men lift "holy hands, without wrath and debate (dispute)"; that women *"in like manner"* be adorned "modestly and with sound mind" "by good deeds, as befits women who profess religion" [vv 8-10]. In such an environment, the women should learn in "silence."

As has happened with other words we have discussed, "silence" may be an unfortunate choice of an English word. Looking at different lexicons (sort of like dictionaries, but which survey how a word is used), the sense is not so much "don't open your mouth." Rather it indicates the temperament of a "God-produced calm which includes an inner tranquility that supports appropriate action."[37]

Paul uses basically the same word for those who "work in *quietness* and eat their own bread" [II Thessalonians 3:12]. When a Jewish riot is fomenting, Paul is permitted to address them in Hebrew, at which "they kept all the more *silent*" [Acts 22:2] – that is, rather than prolonging the uproar, they stop to pay close attention to what he is saying. In fact, earlier in I Timothy 2, Paul urges prayer for "kings and all who are in high positions, that we may lead a quiet and *peaceable* ('silent') life, godly and respectful in every way" [v 2]. This would also seem to be St Peter's frame of mind when he says, "rather let it be the hidden person of the heart, with the incorruptible beauty of a gentle and *quiet* spirit, which in God's sight is very precious" [I Peter 3:4].

In a sense, the English "silence" may be an appropriate word, as for instance to "silence one's heart" or to "silence one's mind," which would reflect more the mind at ease, the heart contented, the freedom from

128

rebellion, and the openness to learn and grow. But this is not in the way that we normally use it and therefore it can have a misleading interpretation.

A Different "Silent"

I Corinthians 14, however, has a contrasting concept with a *different* word: Paul is just finishing a discussion in regard to how "God is not the Author of *confusion* but of *peace*" [v 33], and then adds

> Let the women in the churches be silent, for it is not permitted to them to speak; but are to be in submission, as the law also says. If they want to learn anything, let them ask their own husbands at home; for it is a shame for women to speak in church.   vv 34-35

Here, the word for "silent" is a different one – it does mean in essence, indelicately put, "close your mouth!" But this is a different circumstance. To begin with, remember that in the early Church the people still follow the synagogue seating arrangement, where the women would sit on one side, and the men on the other. When Paul says "if they want to learn something," it would seem that he is addressing a situation where some women are asking questions, possibly of their neighbors or of their husbands *on the other side of the group*, and disrupting the worship. Therefore comes the admonition that they should "ask their own husbands *at home*."

So, whereas this "silent" deals with outer disruption and therefore is cause to admonish that one should "close the mouth," the "silence" of I Timothy rather emphasizes "the inner God-produced calm," which provides an atmosphere within the congregation fertile for learning.

Authority Over the Man

Still, in I Timothy 2:12, Paul adds, "I do not permit a woman ... to have authority over a man." The word "authority" in the Greek is noteworthy.

This is the only place where it appears in the New Testament, and lexicons indicate that it is quite a harsh word, as according to *Thayer's Greek Lexicon*:

1) one who with his own hands kills another or himself
2) one who acts on his own authority, autocratic
3) an absolute master
4) to govern, exercise dominion over one[38]

Strong's *Exhaustive Concordance* even suggests "domineer over." This then speaks of a usurpation of power, a deliberate perversion of the order of headship, and a conscious rebellion against the humility and mutual submission which Paul emphasizes in Ephesians 5:21. In this context, then, a woman deciding on her own to take on an authority role over men and basically to control the outcome is entirely inappropriate.

Again there must be a balance in understanding. Her commission is to be a real contributor in the joint task of being "the Image of God" – after all, she is "the helper suitable for man" [Genesis 2:18] who is to represent *Jehovah*'s "help" and salvation to the man. No mere onlooker or figurehead, she is rather a co-worker with the man, having a *God-designed* different perspective, with whom the man is to be constantly in reference and in consultation. As mentioned previously, the Lord made no human to be sufficient in and of him/herself. Therefore the man needs her "help" if he is to fulfill his mission to Creation. The design still holds even after the Fall into sin – the Creator's design does not crumble nor is it negated by human rebellion (otherwise man would lose *his* authority as well).

In I Corinthians 11:3-16, Paul discusses when a woman "prays" or "prophesies," which seem to be not private or just familial activities but rather worship-community related activities – that is, *leading in prayer* or *preaching* (more than simply "future-telling," "prophesying" is to reveal the Lord's will in the past, present and/or future). Paul does not forbid the woman these activities, but rather emphasizes that they be done with the proper decorum, which is to acknowledge the sequence of headship so that there is no usurpation of authority, which only leads to confusion and chaos.

Martin Luther comments on this idea:

> Paul did not forbid this out of his own devices, but appealed to the law, which says that women are to be subject (Gen 3:16). From the law Paul was certain that the Spirit was not contradicting Himself by now elevating the woman above the men after He had formerly subjected them to the men; but rather, being mindful of His former institution, He was arousing them to preach, as long as there is no lack of men. How could Paul otherwise have singlehandedly resisted the Holy Spirit, who promised in Joel (2:28): "And your daughters, who all prophesied." "And Miriam the sister of Moses was also a prophetess" (Exod 15:20). And Uldah the prophetess gave advice to pious King Josiah (II Kings 22:14-20), and Deborah did the same to Duke Barak (Judges 4:4-7); and finally the song of the Virgin Mary (Luke 1:46-55) is praised throughout the world. Paul himself in I Cor 11:5 instructs the women to pray and prophecy with covered heads. Therefore order, discipline, and respect demand that women keep silent when men speak; but if no man were to preach, then it would be necessary for the women to preach.
>
> Martin Luther[39]

Teaching and Priscilla

When Paul states, "I do not permit a woman to teach" [I Timothy 2:12] is there a conflict such as Luther identifies?

There is a curious case presented by Aquila and Priscilla [Acts 18:2, 18, 26; Romans 16:3; I Corinthians 16:19; II Timothy 4:19]. They are introduced in the standard ancient practice, which always mentions the man first, then the woman. But then, except for I Corinthians, Priscilla is afterwards mentioned first[40], even when this team shows Apollos "more accurately the Way of God" [Acts 18:26]. As a comparison, in Acts, up unto the first missionary journey, whenever Barnabas and Paul are discussed, Barnabas is mentioned first, which would indicate that he is the lead person with his "assistant" Paul/Saul. But as the first missionary journey begins, soon it becomes "Paul and his party" [Acts 3:13] and "Paul and Barnabas" [v 43], indicating that the lead person is now Paul. So, when Priscilla is mentioned first, is it because she is the lead person in their ministry, possibly having the greater *gift* for *their* work – is she in the ranks of Deborah and the other women Luther mentioned? If so, would her using her gift be because she has decided to "do her own thing," or would she have proceeded in respect to the principle of headship identified in the last chapter?

What Does "Helper" Mean?

Just how does the statement "the helper suitable for man" apply here, especially since this "God's help" is not merely physical help, but also the essential second spiritual perspective for a binocular view of God? If a woman can have greater expertise in a certain area than the man, in mutual submission, would – should – the man defer to her who has the greater knowledge and background rather than proving his ignorance? Should a man who has no medical education learn from a woman who is trained in that profession? Can a woman who has studied and can present sound arguments in regard to doctrines be a useful resource as "God's help" to the man, providing valuable insight and teaching?

Indeed, there is no question that a woman can be very capable! Proverbs 31:10-31 describes a most competent, knowledgeable and industrious woman. She is a very important contributor to the life, spirituality, welfare and strength of her family as she makes decisions, carries on business and directs her servants on her own. Humorously, the comment has been made in reference to her husband sitting in the gates with the elders [v 23], that there is nothing else left for him to do. Although she is presented as an ideal, this passage indicates that a woman can certainly be very proficient and still not violate the headship sequence – there is no usurping nor domineering, but instead a true contributing to the well-being and livelihood of the family.

When Paul speaks of a woman "praying" or "prophesying," he maintains that such delegation of authority should be clearly identified (he speaks of "the head covered" as symbol of the chain of authority [I Corinthians 11:3-10]) so that there is no confusion and misunderstanding as to what is happening. Although the principle, following the concept of headship, is that a woman normally listens "in quietness of mind," are there times when God occasionally does things which are "not normal"? A virgin birth, for example? And if we allow for this and do not overstep the sequence of headship, would it be a recognition of God's gifting of both the male and the female?

However, it should also be pointed out that while the woman can be so capable, this does not warrant the man abdicating his importance in the life and spirituality of the family. God has shown that His intentional chief point of contact with the family and with humanity is through the man. Although it is the men who are instructed to bring up the children "in the training and admonition of the Lord" [Ephesians 6:4; see Proverbs 4:1-4; Isaiah 38:19], too often the men have left that for the women to do, thereby indicating that religion is not a "manly" thing. Perhaps some men do not intend to suggest this, but what they fail to realize is that every action they do, every word they speak, every attitude they express is constantly teaching their children. Despite how capable the woman may be, the man cannot defer his responsibility.

Challenge

"Headship" is an issue with which human nature is uncomfortable, not only because of its abuse, but also just because it exists. It is not, however, a put-down of women or of their capability, it is simply one method of the Creator reflecting Himself in humanity.

As when in John 6, Jesus makes statements that cause some to be offended and walk "with Him no more," some will take offense, no matter what Jehovah may declare, merely because He was the One Who declared it. Some reject God's ultimate say over what He designed, or believing instead that He has become passé based on our "new and improved" concept of humanity. We will take Him when He is convenient, but will we turn away when He describes what runs counter to the philosophy du jour?

Paul is not "anti-woman," but rather he works very hard to identify what are God's principles. He reminds us that there are some things that are inescapable if one is to follow the Bible – for example, that the woman was created for the sake of man. However, he then also reminds us:

> Nevertheless, neither is man independent of woman, nor woman independent of man, in the Lord. For as woman is from man, even so man also comes through woman; *and all things are from God.*
> I Corinthians 11:11-12

There is a balance to be kept in mind and, ultimately, we all kneel at the feet of our God – in the "silence" of I Timothy 2.

12. Nakedness (Transparency)

The man and his wife were both naked, and were not ashamed.

Genesis 2:25

"Naked" is another of those "before" and "after" words. Like "subdue," it has one meaning before the Fall into sin, as the description of innocence, but afterwards it is the portrait of guilt and therefore of shame. It is the focal point in the cost of Adam and Eve's rebellion and of their rejection of God's will [Genesis 3:7, 10-11].

"Naked" – Before

This is more than merely body image and sex consciousness. Since the stated purpose for the creation – for the existence – of humankind is "the Image of God" [Genesis 1:26], therefore the context of "nakedness" is set within humanity's relationship *to Jehovah*, not with each other.

After all, before the Fall, physical modesty really would have no bearing since they were the only two people around. They would have no reason for disguise nor concealment, not toward God, not toward each other, and certainly not toward the rest of Creation.[41] It might even be called "transparency." It is the difference of having such a clean mirror, that Adam and Eve might be ask, "Can you see Him now? How is the picture of the Creator now?" The "naked" mirror has no fogginess, nor distortion, nor misdirection in regard to "the Image" which it bears.

This is expressed most beautifully in Exodus 33:11, when God talks with Moses 'face-to-face as with a friend.' Here is a glimpse of the relationship that was the Creator's intention when He first formed the man and made the human so pivotal in regard to His activity on the earth. Here is the fellowship represented by "the sound of Jehovah God walking in the garden in the cool of the day" [Genesis 3:8], the companionship of Covenant which we later see with Abraham. Here is the intimacy of Moses asking 'Please, show me Your Glory' [Exodus 33:18] and of the Lord revealing His innermost identity.

The Hebrew root for "naked" in its positive, therefore pre-Fall, emphasis is "prudent" or "sensible," a concept connected with "to know," and there seems to be a certain irony, perhaps chosen precisely to indicate that both the man and the woman were adequately equipped to withstand the lies and temptations of Satan:

> The prudent one does not vaunt his knowledge, (Prov 12:23) ignores an insult, (Prov 12:16) acts with knowledge, (Prov 14:8) looks where he is going, (Prov 14:15) sees danger and acts appropriately (Prov 22:3 = Prov 27:12), and is crowned with knowledge.(Prov 14:18)   *TWOT*[42]

Living "the Image"

When Jehovah describes His Glory as His "goodness, Covenant, grace, mercy, Steadfast Love, faithfulness, forgiveness and justice," he sets before His humans the essential content of what His Image is to be.

Therefore the two in their "nakedness" will express these qualities: the woman, emphasizing the nurturing of God, is to set an environment of love, mercy and grace which envelops a child from infancy to adulthood[43]; and as "the mother of all living," this extends toward all Creation as well. Meanwhile, the man also is to exhibit "love, mercy and grace" in regard to the dominion of the Creator:

> ... as the writer Armstrong Williams remarks in the article *The Definition of Father*, "...every father must take the time to be a dad as well as a friend, disciplinarian, shoulder to cry on, dance partner, coach, audience, adviser, listener, and so much more." Williams, the writer quoted above,

136

goes on to say that he viewed his father as the driving force in his family and also someone who brought strength and compassion to his family.[44]

Neither the masculine nor the feminine traits deal with brutality, injustice, aggression, insensitivity and the like. These results of a self-centered "power trip" are a most visible demonstration of the rebellion of sin and have nothing to do with "the Image" that is to be expressed. Instead consider the challenge which Jesus gives especially to men, "that you may be sons of your Father in heaven":

> But I say to you: Love your enemies, bless those who curse you, do nobly to those who hate you, and pray for those who abuse you and persecute you, that you may be sons of your Father in heaven; because He makes His sun rise on the evil and on the good, and sends rain on the righteous and on the unrighteous. Matthew 5:44-45

> But Love your enemies, do good, and lend, not at all despairing; your reward will be great, and you will be sons of the Most High, for He is kind to the ungrateful and evil. You be compassionate, just as your Father also is compassionate. Luke 6:35-36

Is this the way God carries out the dominion of the universe? Really?

> God asserts His Love for us in that while we were *still sinners* Christ died for us. ... *while we were enemies* we were reconciled to God by the death of his Son, much more, having been reconciled, we shall be saved by His life. Romans 5:8,10

Yes, Jehovah has control; yes, Jehovah, has discipline; yes, Jehovah has to stand forcefully against the rebellion that destroys His Creation – and yet He is also a God Who will give the ultimate sacrifice of Himself *for His enemies!* He will not treat rejection trivially, He will not applaud injustice, He will not blindly support the selfish whims of people – and yet look at how He will not be derailed when He sets out to give them the opportunity to receive His eternal blessings! If the man and the woman are to give the universe a glimpse of *this* God, their work is certainly cut out for them.

The Attributes of "the Image"

We need to closely examine the attributes of "the Glory" because these are the elements which are to be clearly seen in the "naked" "Image of God."

Goodness

The Moving Human Target of "Goodness"

In the first place, a solid base is needed to determine "goodness." Satan's temptation to Adam and Eve is that they would "know good and evil." They already know what is right and wrong, so what they are offered is more than just an experience of "good and evil," but rather the intimate knowledge by which "good and evil" is *defined*. What is "good" for Adam would be "good"; and what is "good" for Eve would be "good." However, this does not guarantee that the two "goods" would be the same. Isaiah in his famous chapter 53 says, "All we like sheep have gone astray; each of us has turned to his own path" [v 6]. So if I steal your car, that is "good" – for me – although you may not agree with that assessment.

When there is no standard, then a person determines what is good "in his own eyes." Proverbs has strong words for such a situation: "Do you see a man wise in his own eyes? There is more hope for a fool than for him" [Proverbs 26:12]; and "A generation pure in its own eyes is not washed from its filthiness" [Proverbs 30:12]. And finally, declared twice: "There is a way that appears upright before a man, but its result is the way of death" [Proverbs 14:12; 16:25].

The Anarchic Ideal of "Goodness"

Considering history over the last decade, where those on Wall Street gave themselves extravagant bonuses in the wake of a major financial crash that decimated many people's futures; where politicians are quick to follow those who will contribute the most to their re-election funds, but cannot hear the cries of their constituents; where rulers and their armies are willing to slaughter their own people in order to maintain their power; where people speed down a road known for its deadly crashes, tossing off speeding fines because "I can make that much in a few hours of work"; where a clique of teenagers text-bully a person because it is fun and gives them a sense of power – even depending on a general consensus of what is "good" can be a worrisome thing.

The list goes on throughout history: the French revolution and its guillotine; the Nazi regime with its "brown shirts" and its pogroms against Jews, gypsies, and Christians; the Communist reigns in Russia and China with their "disposal" of unwanteds, and their gulags and re-education camps – all of these have demonstrated how easily and quickly the common person's concept of "good" can be skewed into terrible proportions. As this writer's father used to comment, when the Lord calls us "sheep" it is not a compliment. In fact, consult Moses as to whether he agrees with "Vox Populi, Vox Dei" ("the voice of the people is the voice of God") – it seems that he dealt with a number of popular rebellions as he led Israel through to the Covenant Land.

Consider our culture's fascination with violence in electronic games and in sports; yet on the other hand there is a "cocooning" attitude where people retreat into the safety and security of their homes because of fear, where more and more they limit themselves to a virtual and controllable world. Consider the fixation of the advertising and the entertainment world on sex "because it sells," as it erodes a most significant of human relationships into mere recreation. Even the terminology has been turned inside out – for example, when something is "bad" or "wicked" it really is "good." Of course, this is not new:

> Woe to those who call evil good, and good evil; who put darkness for light, and light for darkness; who put bitter for sweet, and sweet for bitter!   Isaiah 5:20

Just what effect do these trends have on the common concept of what is "good"? What is happening to the value system out of which humans judge what is "good"? Why do we choose negative terminology where there is – or should be – an abundance of positive words?

Coming Full Circle to "Goodness"

In the other attributes encompassed by the Creator's Glory as stated in Exodus 33 and 34, we recognize an elegant working definition of "goodness" – again: covenant relationship, grace, mercy, Steadfast Love, faithfulness, forgiveness, and justice. The purest form of these attributes can be found only in Jehovah Himself – in other words, we discover that by looking to "the Original" for our "Image of God," we can determine a solid basis for "goodness": "Do not be wise in your own eyes; fear Jehovah and depart from evil" [3:7] or as Jesus identifies it: "No one is good except God alone" [Mark 10:18].

"Good" is what the Creator is and does as was expressed in Genesis 1. The intent of this "goodness" is what He declares in Jeremiah: "For I know the thoughts that I think toward you, says Jehovah, thoughts of peace and not of evil, to give you a future and a hope" [Jeremiah 29:11]. His "goodness" ultimately results in "salvation" [II Timothy 1:9; Titus 3:5] and "abundant life" [John 10:10] When He moves into our world and into

140

human flesh itself, not for His own benefit but to die on the Cross for those who are in rebellion against Him, this is where "goodness" takes on a depth that demonstrates how empty are the human one-sided concepts of "goodness."

The Risk of God's "Goodness"

There are those who criticize how a "good" God can allow suffering. Unfortunately that will have to be – and has been, from other sources – a book of its own. It is not an answer that can be given "in just enough words to fit on a bumper sticker." Still, an essential understanding requires us to find where the responsibility does lie:

> Yet might one wonder if there is bit of hypocrisy in the background of this question. Humans want the luxury of "free will," but if one is not allowed to exercise it when it brings suffering to others, then what is the point of such "free will"? There is little, if any, human rebellion against God that does not affect others in some negative way. Or should the impact be rated so that *this* kind of result to *this* degree is permissible, but the Lord cannot allow anything beyond *that* degree? Yet the consequence may be subtle, perhaps in gradually eroding another person's self-confidence, so that at first it does not seem so bad and yet farther down the line the results are devastating. Who then will set the standards that God must follow?   James Lindemann[45]

> At first our human nature immediately accuses God of mismanaging the universe, but we then stand under the hypocrisy of demanding free will and yet condemning God for the results of the choices that humans make. We tend to overlook that it is not God Who holds the bloody knife, but rather humans that do.   James Lindemann[46]

As identified earlier, because of human rebellion, Creation also has lost its anchor:

> For in earnest expectation, Creation expectantly awaits the revealing of the sons of God. For Creation was subjected to aimlessness and corruption, not voluntarily, but because of Him Who subjected it in hope; because the Creation also will be freed from the slavery of

corruption into the freedom of the Glory of the children of God. For we know that the whole Creation groans and travails together until now.

Romans 8:19-22

The "goodness" of God allowed humans to have free choice so that they may truly love and not merely be puppets on a string. It involved taking the risk that the wrong choice may be made, which is what humans have done. Although that wrong choice has brought all kinds of brokenness and suffering into Creation, the "goodness" of God surprisingly, willingly shoulders the burden:

> Surely He has borne our calamities and carried our agonies; yet we judged Him as punished, struck by God, and oppressed. But He was wounded for our rebellion, He was crushed for our iniquities; the chastisement for our peace was upon Him, and by His stripes we are healed. Isaiah 53:4-5

In other words, the definition of "goodness" and the answer to the suffering of the world is to be found in the Baby in the manger and the King of the Jews dying upon a Cross – in the Jehovah Who did not stumble at becoming personally involved, in the God Who would go the extreme distance for His Creation.

Covenant Relationship

This is one of the most important topics in the Bible, under which this writer has a more in-depth discussion in another book, *Covenant: The Blood is the Life*[47]. As referred to earlier in chapter 2, it is a significant relationship which is begun in the man's creation, a Blood/Soul/Life connection, in which he would be "the Image of God."

Despite the Fall into sin, this kind of connection is particularly reflected in Jehovah's bond to Abraham, the distinctive Covenant that dominates the Old Testament. It is an intimate closeness which extends beyond this man and down throughout his offspring even to today. When we look at the following attributes of God's Glory in the following sections, we see them repeatedly in this relationship, even when we are puzzled why Jehovah would hold so unbreakably to Covenant, yet such is the strength and comfort which this bond holds. It is within this context that God is willing to give the ultimate sacrifice for this Covenant People's sakes, as we read in the prophets, and yet the effects are so powerful that all of humanity can receive these benefits:

> He says, "It is too trifling that You should be My Servant to raise up the tribes of Jacob, and to restore the preserved ones of Israel! I will give You as a Light to the nations, to be My Salvation to the ends of the earth."
> Isaiah 49:6

It is a relationship which God takes most seriously and even when He must severely discipline His People, century upon century He refuses to break the Covenant although He has much cause – until He speaks prophetically through Zechariah:

> I took my staff, Kindness/Grace, and cut it in two, that I might break My Covenant which I had cut with all the peoples – it was broken in that day. So the afflicted of the flock, who were watching Me, knew that it was the Word of Jehovah.
> Then I said to them, "If it is good in your eyes, give me My wages; and if not, let it go." So they weighed out for My wages thirty pieces of silver. Jehovah said to Me, "Throw it to the potter" – that magnificent price at which I was valued. So I took the thirty pieces of silver and threw them into the house of Jehovah for the potter.
> 11:10-13

The second paragraph sets the context of the breaking of Covenant at the death of Jesus. In Genesis 15:17, Jehovah, as "a smoking furnace and torch of fire," had passed between the pieces of animals cut in half, a ritual commonly understood in that culture as the pledge of death should one break Covenant. Now that pledge "comes home to roost" on the Cross.

Yet in that very same death a new Covenant is born, "This Cup is the New Covenant in My Blood, which is poured out for you" [Luke 22:20].

Here, in the New Covenant, there is an even greater intimacy, as the Holy Spirit makes His home in us [John 14:17, 23; I Corinthians 6:19], and through Holy Communion, Jesus gives of His Flesh and Soul (Blood) which enters us and becomes one with us. In the New Covenant, "the Glory of God" only intensifies.

Grace

When Jehovah chooses Abram (Abraham) [Genesis 12:1-5], there is nothing in the text to indicate anything about the spiritual state of the man, even whether he believes in Jehovah at that time or not. He is selected as the root that would eventually bear the Savior simply because God decides to give him that honor. Even those who would become heroes of faith — Jacob, Moses, Gideon, Samson and others — are not chosen because of how their life and faith could impress God, but rather the Lord singles them out and turns them into His stars.

Of course, "grace" would reach its climax as Jesus sacrifices Himself not just for future believers, but for the whole world, even those who will go to their graves in rebellion. We see the hard and gritty road that this attribute is willing to travel because the Lord holds on to a Covenant to which He has committed Himself. He holds fast to Israel throughout centuries of their abuse and rebellion, even when the physical presence of God in Jesus is rejected, even, in fact, when they attempt to eliminate Him on the Cross. Even in this He does not rightfully annihilate, but rather He saves. That is the definition of "grace."

Mercy

"Mercy" and "grace" are often treated together, yet they are not the same. "Mercy" stretches out its hand to someone in desperate need (even when he/she may not realize how desperate the situation is), while "grace" says that although it does not have to – there is no way its object can compel an act of grace, in fact, that object even may be vehemently resisting – "grace" chooses to show this "mercy" anyway. As we see these two working together in the above paragraphs, we find that "binocular" view of Jehovah again, where both occur simultaneously, neither by happenstance, but together they reveal a powerful chosen commitment to save those in need.

Steadfast Love

The Hebrew term is *"Hesed"* and as one considers its profound concept of Love in relation to Covenant, one wonders "which came first, the chicken or the egg?" Does Covenant arise out of the desire to express a most determined and deep-rooted Love, or is Love the compelling result of a bond and commitment as intimate and total as Covenant?

> Glueck makes something of I Sam 20:8,14,15 where David and Jonathan swore friendship. This covenant, says G. was the basis of the hesed. Here, perhaps, is G's major mistake. He forgets that covenants arise on the basis of a relationship and that the obligations are often deeper than the covenant. Verse 17 shows that Jonathan's love moved him to make the covenant. When Jonathan died, David lamented for him out of love, not obligation. (II Sam 1:26). David's hesed to Saul's house is said to be for the sake of Jonathan, not because of a legal obligation. (II Sam 9:1,3,7) …
>
> … It does not follow that God's love is merely a factor in a covenant; rather the covenant is the sign and expression of his love…
>
> Another pair of nouns is covenant [berît] and hesed used seven times with some other instances of use in near contexts. The main instance is Deut 7:9,12 which has echoes in I Kgs 8:23; II Chr 6:14; Neh 1:5;9:32; and Dan 9:4. It itself is called by Stoebe (THAT, p. 616) a paraphrase of Ex 34:6. He remarks that Deut 7:8 ready bases all God's

favor on his love. If this pair be translated 'covenantal love' or 'covenant and love,' it should be remembered that the love is back of the covenant. This point is illustrated by Jer 2:2 where the hesed of Israel's youth is likened to the love of a bride. The love of a bride is the basis of the promise, not the result. *TWOT*[48]

Or in the case of Jehovah, do they simply occur concurrently because *they must*, and therefore also seamlessly enhance each other?

Although, for example, the vow of marriage (Covenant) takes place out of the Love which a couple has for each other, there are times, least humanly speaking, when that vow also upholds Love during times of stress – even a long-term stress which tests the "steadfastness" of the Love. The husband faithfully comes each day to help feed his dementia-afflicted wife, because "after all, that is what I promised when we got married – in sickness and in health!" Part of the endurance of Steadfast Love is that one also sets up guards and supports in order that its determined nature remains true.

This is a reflection of the Creator doing the same thing, He Who created Covenant from the very opening chapters of Genesis, He Who because of Love can also say, "because of Covenant, I will ...":

> For their sake He remembered His Covenant, and sighed in compassion according to the abundance of His Steadfast Love. Psalm 106:45

> He has remembered His Covenant forever, the Word which He commanded, for a thousand generations Psalm 105:8

And also this Covenant gives us the ability to claim His love, based on His Covenant, His Glory, His Name:

> Do not abhor us, for Your Name's sake; do not disgrace the throne of Your Glory. Remember!! Do not break Your Covenant with us!
> Jeremiah 14:21

Faithfulness (Truth)

This reminds us of the above section, "I Plight Thee My Troth,"[49] in which we see the man, reflecting "the Original's" commitment, pledging his "truth [or fidelity]" to his bride. What is intriguing is that the word for "Faithfulness" in Hebrew is a form of the word for "Truth," so that marriage's "fidelity and truth" can claim a heritage that goes back to the oldest books of the Bible.

As is becoming apparent, these qualities which we are discussing do not have sharp boundaries between each other. This should not be surprising since they all come from the Source of Jehovah's heart. Therefore "Steadfast Love" cannot but help walk hand-in-hand with "Faithfulness." Jehovah will accomplish what He vows, He will fulfill what He promises, He will carry out the desire of His heart.

Once, as Pilate watched his own ethics and the ethics of the Roman standards slowly crumble before the will of the Jewish leaders, he cynically asked, "What is 'truth'?" [John 18:38]. That is actually a good question, at the same level as "What is 'good'?" Jesus, though, has already given the answer: "I am the Way, the Truth, and the Life" [John 14:6] – Pilate wants a formula, but what Jesus offers is a Person. The "Truth" is what Jesus *is*, which is what God *is*. Abruptly we find ourselves back in the "Headship" discussion, along with "the Image of God," where Jesus, by reflecting His Head, reveals what God is and what He is about. The man, and the woman, are then also to be "the truth" as they in turn reflect Jesus, Who He is and what He is about. They are to accurately reflect the commitment, consistency, and heart-nature of their "Original" – they are not only to reflect the faithfulness of God, but also to be a faithful reflection of the nature of God.

Justice (Judgment)

"Justice" can mean the fair, or appropriate, distribution of a certain asset – or liability. In a sense, that idea is really not far from God's "justice," although the result may be uncomfortable.

All humans desire a favoritism of some sort, where we receive preferential treatment, perhaps because of our best behavior or religious fervor. St Paul puts it this way:

> Even I could have confidence in the flesh – if anyone thinks there is confidence in the flesh, I more so:
>   circumcised the eighth day,
>   of the nation of Israel,
>   of the tribe of Benjamin,
>   a Hebrew born of the Hebrews;
>   according to the Law, a Pharisee;
>   according to zeal, persecuting the Church;
>   according to the righteousness which is in the Law, blameless.
>   But what things were gain to me, these I have counted loss for Christ. … count them as garbage, that I may gain Christ
>
> Philippians 3:4-8

Paul realizes that God will have no favoritism because His standards find in us no difference:

for all have sinned and come short of the Glory of God   Romans 3:23

But the Scripture has imprisoned all under sin   Galatians 3:22

For there is not a righteous man on earth who does good and never sins.
Ecclesiastes 7:20

God's "justice" then means that all receive the same judgment, not an "asset" but the same "liability," which God identified already in the first chapters of the Bible as the condemnation of death [Genesis 2:17], a judgment which still exists in the New Testament: "For the wages of sin is death" [Romans 6:23]. In rebellion, humanity has withdrawn from its

Creator and therefore is forfeit life – and it is forfeit His help, His protection, with so much more. Humankind stands vulnerable and without defense from fellow humans and from a Creation that no longer has the stabilizing "Image of God" to depend on.

God's call is for us to repent, but some will persistent in their rebellion – as the saying puts it, they keep hitting their head against the wall "because it feels so good when they stop." Some people object to "hell" because it is such a cruel thing, and it is. But in a real sense it is simply a natural result of their own rebellion and rejection of the Source of Life – they have built it themselves. Jesus describes it as "outer darkness; there will be weeping and gnashing of teeth" [Matthew 8:12; 22:13; 24:51; 25:30] – not from true repentance ("Godly sorrow brings a repentance that leads to salvation and has no regret, but worldly sorrow brings death" [II Corinthians 7:10]), but rather in the anger and hatred because they have received the result of their own attitudes, while never admitting that it is indeed their own fault. Adam's attitude of "but it wasn't *my* fault" ("The woman whom *You* gave to be with me, *she* gave me of the tree ..." [Genesis 3:12]) will live on into eternity.

Sadly, the rebellion – and its judgment – often persists in the family: "the iniquity of the fathers upon the children and the children's children to the third and the fourth generation" [Exodus 34:7] – as is most markedly seen in family abuse and in other rebellions that descend through generations.

There is a tough aspect to "the Image of God" in which the human is to "not pervert justice; ... not show partiality, nor take a bribe" [Deuteronomy 16:19]. The Lord requires us to reflect Him: to be fair, but moreover to stand firm in condemnation where there is wrong.

Forgiveness

To understand the heart of Jehovah in regard to condemnation as well as forgiveness, there is an important story in Genesis 18: God comes calling on Abraham. The chapters previous to this event are necessary to set the background. In Chapter 15 and 17, the Lord and Abraham have completed the Covenant basic to the identity of what will be the Covenant People – the Circumcision Covenant. As Covenant goes, the unity of the Blood/Soul/Life means particularly that the Creator's "Blood" now flows through Abraham – the very Soul of God is in Abraham's veins.

God comes specifically looking for an intercessor – as Jesus has become for us. He reveals to Abraham that He must come in judgment against Sodom and Gomorrah, "Because the outcry against Sodom and Gomorrah is great, and because their sin is very grave" [v 20]. Abraham rises to the task and argues on behalf of the condemned, but it is not *he* who is arguing, it is the "Blood/Soul/Life" that runs in his veins that is arguing – in vivid display, the Love of God in "the Image of God" is arguing with the Justice of God. What is made visible is Jehovah's inner struggle when He must come in judgment.

And observe what happens! God's Justice bends over backwards to the point where it should fall over! "Sodom and Gomorrah" make up a territory including five cities [14:8]. Of the thousands living in this territory, look at what Jehovah says, "If I find in Sodom fifty righteous within the city, I will spare *the whole place on their account*" [18:26] – even all those against whom "the outcry" was made! And then, when Abraham is finished, the number is down to only ten. When we number Lot, his wife and two unmarried daughters[50] among the ten, then how pathetic that there were not found *six* more in that territory! – out of how many thousands??

How near forgiveness is, but when His grace and mercy are rejected, then in the end God will be Just – and judgment is indeed visited upon the territory.

We have seen the heart of God, even when it must break by visiting judgment upon those who rebel. Yet when there is repentance, then, as in no other religion, what is unleashed is a marvelous set of powerful images concerning forgiveness. For example, in the *Yom Kippur* (Day of Atonement) ritual, the sins of the people are confessed on the head of "the scapegoat," which then is driven into the wilderness [Leviticus 16:21-22]. Supposedly there are flag-bearers stationed along the route who would wave their flag as the goat passes by – which, if true, would give an effective and electrifying visual backdrop to the Psalmist's "As far as the east is from the west, so far has He removed our transgressions from us" [Psalm 103:12]. Other graphic descriptions of forgiveness include:

> He will have compassion on us, and He will bring our iniquities into subjection. You will cast all our sins into the depths of the sea.
> Micah 7:19

> You loved my soul from the pit of destruction, You have cast all my sins behind Your back
> Isaiah 38:17

The sacrifices also would allow the repentant to be shown the forgiveness of sins and the restoration to life. Yet there is the problem that the sins keep returning – "It is impossible for the Blood of bulls and goats to take away sins" [Hebrews 10:4]. Therefore the last image is the most amazing of all, as on a Cross the Judge Himself suffers the sentence of condemnation in full:

> For Christ died for sins once for all, the Righteous for the unrighteous, to bring you to God.
> I Peter 3:18

which now allows God to declare:

I, I am He Who blots out your transgressions for My own sake; and your sins I will not remember. Isaiah 43:25

For I will forgive their iniquity, and will not again remember their sin.
Jeremiah 31:34

This then is the forgiveness that "the Image of God" is called upon to emulate in men and women's lives because there is no other way for Creation to experience this quality of the Creator's Glory.

Transparency

Again, the frustration is to try to identify what the rebellion-less Adam and Eve must be like as they are naked – fully transparent – for the qualities of Jehovah's Glory to be reflected unhindered in them. Unfortunately our explanations cannot do that. Instead since we come from a severely sin-distorted reflection within a thoroughly sin-polluted spiritual environment, we are simply left with describing something we just do not know.

13. Nakedness (Guilt)

"As in a Mirror Indistinctly" [I Corinthians 13:12]

Although glass was already around for centuries, apparently the method to make *clear* glass (but as yet with poor optical quality) was not discovered until around 100 AD, a bit too late for St Paul to use it as the metaphor in this quote. Still, putting that aside, the quote does introduce an interesting (although modern) analogy. Switching from a mirror concept to a window concept, humanity is to be a window by which the hidden God is made visible. When sin entered, it was like darkening the glass. The image which should have been showing becomes more and more obscure, while the reflections from our side of the glass become much more noticeable. In some instances it can be hard to distinguish which is from this side and which is from the other side of the window. Sometimes the reflection from our side fully takes over.

"Naked" Sin

In a similar way, when Adam and Eve look for the familiar "Image of God," another image now interferes – their own image. Discovering themselves, they become self-conscious, which is probably a source of fascination at first. But there is something else that becomes quickly apparent: none of the beauty of "the Glory of God" is found in this new image. What has so "dressed" them before is now *barely* visible if at all – there is an emptiness, a "nakedness" [Genesis 3:7] which has become most obvious. Without the beauty of "the Glory," they discover an ugly blemish, or perhaps a better word is cancer, which dominates this image – there is now a most unpleasant selfishness filling the image. It has not the wonderfulness which had been expected. In fact, it is downright embarrassing.

In the Twinkling of the Eye

As mentioned previously, the root for "naked" can mean "prudent" or "sensible," and one may be curious as how much thought goes into any decision to rebel. Even today we are so often quick to take what seems to be a good idea, only to discover that had we only given it more thought, we would not be in the mess that has resulted. Such far-reaching effects can so easily happen from the act in "a twinkling of the eye."

Another problem that so often occurs is the attitude of "Because I can, therefore I will." Many have said or done something that was very inappropriate based on a moment's thought, and have utterly regretted it for the rest of their lives. It may have been intended as something funny, or a prank, or some such thing, yet people have lost jobs; politicians have ended up in hot water; media (for example, radio) personalities have felt the tide of public approval turn strongly against them.

Rebellion can seem so appealing ("So when the woman saw that the tree was good for food, that it was pleasant to the eyes, and a tree desirable to make one wise" [3:6]); it can be so easy ("she took of its fruit"); it can take only a moment ("and ate"); it can be so eagerly shared ("She also gave to her husband with her, and he ate"); and yet the effects relentlessly spread and brought about a terrible result ("through one man sin entered the world, and death through sin, and thus death spread to all men, because all sinned" [Romans 5:12]).

Shame

The result of all this is that for the first time in history, "shame" makes its appearance. This word has the most telling of associations:

> The primary meaning of this root is 'to fall into disgrace, normally through failure, either of self or of an object of trust.' ... The word is often paralleled with ... 'to be humiliated,' and less frequently with ... 'to be shattered, dismayed.' ... the English stresses the inner attitude, the state of mind, while the Hebrew means 'to come to shame' and stresses the sense of public disgrace, a physical state. ...
>
> The second usage of *[shame]* expresses that sense of confusion, embarrassment, and dismay when matters turn out contrary to one's expectations. Thus, Job speaks of the shame of the caravaneers when they do not find water in the expected place. (Job 6:20) ... In a more profound sense, Israel and the nations will be shamed by their idols when they fail them. (Isa 42:17; Jer 22:22; Hos 10:6)
>
> The third usage [carries] ... the disgrace which is the result of defeat at the hands of an enemy ... In particular, the awful shame of being paraded as captives is thought of (Mic 1:11; cf. also Jer 2:26). Involved here are all the nuances of confusion, disillusionment, humiliation, and brokenness which the word connotes. ...
>
> Fourthly, shame results from imprudent or immoral action ... Joab accused David of not thinking things through and thus acting foolishly (II Sam 19:5 [H 6]) ... All the occurrences are ... in references which describe explicitly or implicitly the actions of those who bring disgrace upon their parents or spouses. (Prov 10:5; Prov 12:4; Prov 14:35; etc.)
>
> The final use of *[shame]* is the one which coincides most closely with the common English connotation: a feeling of guilt from having done what is wrong. Jeremiah (6:15) is horrified that the people are not ashamed having committed abomination (idolatry). Similarly, Ezekiel (16:63) indicates that God's grace, manifested in the restoration, will not allay, but increase Judah's sense of shame. Not until then will she see what a terrible thing it was to trust idols instead of the living God. Ezra, discovering the situation in Jerusalem, cries out that he is ashamed because 'our iniquities are higher than our heads.' *TWOT*[51]

Each of the associations has application to Adam and Eve after the Fall: there is confusion and embarrassment since the expected benefits backfired; they are defeated and now are humiliated *slaves* of sin [John 8:34; Romans

7:15-25]; they have acted foolishly and have disgraced each other; and there is the guilt that they attempt to cover, even though they are unwilling to admit it (they would rather hide [Genesis 3:9-10]).

Fig Leaves

> The eyes of both were opened, and they knew that they were naked; and they sewed fig leaves together and made themselves aprons.
>
> Genesis 3:7

The fig tree is the only plant mentioned by name in regard to the Garden of Eden. Again a certain irony comes into play when it becomes the humans' choice to cover their sin:

> Since sugar cane was not introduced into the region until the time of Alexander the Great, the fig was an important source of sweetness (Jud 9:11) in Palestine ..., as was honey also. ... to be able to sit under one's own vine and fig tree was to share God's blessings of peace, prosperity and security, whether in past remembrance (I Kgs 4:25 [H 5.5] ...) or in future eschatological hope (Mic 4:4; Zech 3:10).   *TWOT*[52]

In the Bible, the fig represents the "sweet life," and it seems all too modern to see Adam and Eve try to cover the emptiness and destruction of their sin with a thin veneer of "goodness," as they try to convince themselves that that which is sin's result is actually a good and worthwhile thing. The rationalization is akin to that of the Nazi commandant who was guilty of atrocious cruelty, who, because he was "a good family man" and therefore had *some* good in him, some were convinced that he could not be such a monster after all. Whereas his decency toward his family should bring his cruelty into stark relief, it instead was used to mask his deeds.

We want this to work; we want "the covering of fig leaves" to hide the depravity, we want the "goodness" to mitigate the wickedness, we want *any* decency to be enough to redeem the person. After all, this attitude is ultimately self-protection: if we can make it work for him, then there is also hope for us. Then we really do not have to kneel before our Creator in repentance and seek His salvation. Like the child who does her chores *once* and supposes it should cover all the other times which were neglected, or the person who prides himself in having done nothing terribly bad such as robbing a bank, but ignores his daily attitudes, the thin veneer of "goodness" is expected to be "good enough."

The irony in the solution of the leaves is that they are at best temporary: the covering dries up and crumbles away, and what was covered eventually becomes exposed. In fact, like a child who has done something wrong, who acts so obviously with guilt, Adam and Eve, who have been wearing nothing up to this point, now suddenly sport a new clothing fashion as well as hiding when Jehovah visits – even if He were not all-knowing, it would not take a lot of ingenuity for God to recognize that something has drastically changed.

Cunning

> Now the serpent was more cunning than any beast of the field which Jehovah God had made.
> Genesis 3:1

Surprisingly, "cunning" comes from the same word as "naked"! Here in it's negative aspect, "naked" can mean "subtle, shrewd, crafty, cunning, sly." Sadly, this reflects how all the marvelous equipment which God has provided – to Satan before *his* fall, as well as to "the Image of God" (Adam and Eve before their fall) – can quickly be used in a twisted and malicious way. Sadly, the same twistedness is visible down through the years, even and especially now, as God-given knowledge and understanding is used to dismiss Him and His influence over, and partnership with, humanity. For example, Johannes Kepler once described science as "thinking God's thoughts after Him." Now it has become the means by which the world can be destroyed, if not by nuclear holocaust then by pollution, but worse, it also is used to shatter people's faith and hope.

In I Kings 21, Jezebel gets Naboth's vineyard by having him falsely accused of blasphemy. The Jewish leaders tried the same tactic on Jesus but failed until He had to give them what they needed [Matthew 26:59-66]. Balaam, who was hired to curse Israel but instead found himself blessing Israel [Numbers 22-24], still apparently counseled Balak, king of Moab, "to throw a stumbling-block before the sons of Israel, to eat what was sacrificed to idols and to commit sexual immorality" [Revelation 2:14; see Numbers 25:1-3].

So also psychology and statistics are used to influence people's purchases. "Spin doctoring" seeks to give people a false impression of what is said or done. And, of course, "sex sells," whether it be a movie, a perfume, or a car. So also both male and female seek to exploit and seduce for their own gratification. Bullying, peer pressure, and any of many other ways are used in order to compel others to do what is wanted.

The "nakedness" – "cunning" – which has occurred after the Fall is what St Paul contrasts with God's wisdom:

> Where is the wise? Where is the scribe? Where is the debater of this age? Did not God make foolish the wisdom of this world? For, in the wisdom of God, since the world did not know God through wisdom, God was pleased through the foolishness of preaching [the Gospel] to save those who believe.   I Corinthians 1:20-21

The Glory of Man

"Glory" can also be brought into our discussion on this side of the Fall, although it is not God's Glory:

Intimately associated with this third use of [shame] is the question of trust. If Israel seeks to insure her own glory by refusing to trust in God but rather trusts in idols (Isa 1:29) or in foreign nations, (Isa 20:5; 30:3,5) she will not get glory, but shame and disgrace. On the other hand, if one will humbly submit to God, he will find his true glory, for God will not let that person come to shame. (Isa 29:22; Joel 2:26,27; Zeph 3:19) It is this promise of which the Psalmist continually reminds God (Ps 25:3; 31:17 [H 18]; 37:19; 119:46). *TWOT*[53]

Cowardice

Not only do they attempt a thin veneer to cover their sin, not only do they hide in order to avoid the condemnation which they know that they deserve, but now the head of the family resorts to blame: "The woman whom *You* gave to be with me, *she* gave me of the tree ..." [Genesis 3:12]. Thus begins the erosion of integrity and "truth" as "the Image of God" becomes more and more obscured in the humans.

The Glory of God

Already "the Glory of God," as we will come to know it in this fallen universe, comes into play. Although the intimacy with Adam and Eve has been sharply broken, God steps in to give hope. He does not come with the expected condemnation of instant death. He does not abandon these humans with "Well, you made your bed, now lie in it!" He comes – he comes that very day in order to begin the restoration of the pipeline of "Blood/Life/Soul."

He first seeks repentance from the two rebels, which seems to be given howbeit reluctantly. Jehovah does come with curses, but not of the man and the woman! Rather, the Serpent, Satan [Revelation 12:9; 20:2], is cursed, along with Creation (the ground) [Genesis 3:14, 17]. Although vestiges remain, the link between humankind and Creation has been severely damaged.

Yet there is hope: first, there is a promise of a true Helper and Savior Who would come by means of the woman [3:15]; and second, there is a temporary "fix" through the sacrifices, the only source of the skins with which *Jehovah* clothes them [3:21]. A much better "covering" for sin than the fig leaves, they would also point to the more permanent solution of Jesus and the cost which He would have to pay to cover human rebellion.

Driving Adam and Eve out of the Garden is actually also an act of mercy, since if they "take also of the Tree of Life, and eat, and live forever," they would live forever in the hell of their sin. There would be no relief from the wars and rumors of wars, resistance and wrath of nature, and the hopelessness of a condition that would never change. Although cast out, the cherubim would "keep the way to the Tree of Life" [3:24] – "keep" is the same word that is used for Adam's "keeping" the Garden [2:15] and likely indicates to Adam and Eve that the way is not forever closed, but rather "kept" until the Way [John 14:6] comes Who will reopen the path to Life.

And in all of this, Jehovah refuses to stand aloof from His original intent, for such is the yearning of His heart, that time and again He will reestablish and reinforce His Covenant intimacy until the greatest Solution comes and the effect will be forever.

14. The Chief End of Humankind

The Stated Purpose

WESTMINSTER SHORTER CATECHISM

Q. 1. What is the chief end of man?
A. Man's chief end is to glorify God, and to enjoy him forever.[54]

Well ... this is true ... but actually God indicates that He has something even greater in mind: "Let Us make man in Our Image, according to Our [Soul-]Likeness" [Genesis 1:26]. What may be missing in the Catechism's answer is the sense of how Jehovah intends to *express Himself through humanity* to all Creation, even to the angels, since "Do you not know that we are to judge angels?" [II Corinthians 6:3]. The climax of this intent is that a Human (well, a God-Man) now occupies the throne of heaven – and that we will "sit with Him in the heavenly places in Christ Jesus" [Ephesians 2:6]. It does not seem as if Genesis' stated purpose for humanity's existence is to become null on the Last Day.

Of course, the Catechism's answer does become richer if we understand "glorify" according to God's definition of His Glory in Exodus 33 and 34, and that as His Image we are – forever – to reflect the attributes of "goodness, Covenant relationship, grace, mercy, Steadfast Love, faithfulness, forgiveness and justice."

What seems to be missing is that God would enjoy *us* forever "as the bridegroom rejoices over the bride, so shall your God rejoice over you" [Isaiah 62:5]. Heaven is not only described as where we go to be with the Lord, but also how it will be the ultimate "Immanuel" ("God with us"), where Jehovah's desire is to dwell in *our* midst:

I heard a great voice from the throne saying, "Behold, the dwelling of God is with men. He will dwell with them, they will be His People, and God Himself will be their *God with them*"   Revelation 21:3

I will cut with them a Covenant of peace, an everlasting Covenant it shall be with them; I will establish them and multiply them, and I will put My sanctuary in their midst forevermore. My tent shall be with them, and I will be God to them, and they shall be a People to Me.
                                                      Ezekiel 37:26-27

Lasting Consequences

In other words, what we have discussed in this study has eternal ramifications. Because they are expressions of the Creator, male and female characteristics will still be within the heavenly Body of Christ; there will still be submission and headship because it will still exist in the Godhead [I Corinthians 15:25-28]; and we will have a perfect "Soul-Likeness" and "Image of God" since we will experience the fullness of being "in Christ."

The task shared between the man and the woman to make a home not only of the family, particularly the Family of God, but also of the universe, will be reflected in eternity. Unfortunately, it is hard for us to grasp how this will continue after the Last Day, since our sinful state has been more concerned with exploitation than with placing all things under the dominion of the Man (God-Man) Jesus [Ephesians 1:22-23].

Binocular

Remembering how the man and the woman provide the depth which comes from a "binocular" view of God, a reworking of the traits mentioned in the *Stanford Encyclopedia of Philosophy's* feminine ethics article[55] into contrasting groups can be useful in summarizing some of the uniqueness that the genders display about the Lord:

"Male" Traits	"Female" Traits
independence	interdependence
autonomy	community, connection
intellect/*torah*	emotion/passion
wariness (caution, carefulness)	trust
dominion, will	sharing
hierarchy	absence of hierarchy
transcendence	immanence
culture	nature
product	process
rules	relationships
rights	responsibilities
universality	particularity
impartiality	partiality

It must be remembered that this list from the "Feminine Ethics" article identifies how there are differences in approach and even of resolution to ethical dilemmas in contrast to the traditional "male" way of handling such situations, which at times has made the "female" perspective uncomfortable. Is the article flawlessly correct? That is an argument which may be long debated. Yet it is a worthy and perceptive attempt to define how the two points of view spring from different sets of concerns, and therefore is useful in revealing how necessary the "binocular" view is for the "three-dimensional" view of the Creator. As we look at the list, it is important to remember that these are not a list of capacity but rather a list of *concerns* and *viewpoints* – they are the list of what the masculine and the feminine *look for* at *first glance.*

Considering that the man's task involves "subdue," "having dominion," and "headship," the traits listed as "male" really do not come as a great surprise; so also when the woman's task is that of "helper/savior" and "mother" neither are the "female" traits an earthshaker. As each represents point and counterpoint, there is the realization that the balance between the two is not merely useful but essential to truly reflect the true picture of Jehovah to Creation.

So for the one who must lead and take responsibility for the full range of the physical to spiritual welfare of his charge, one indeed can see "independence" and "autonomy" as being essential – and also why the Lord then would rebuke Adam for listening "to your wife" [Genesis 3:17] when he knew better. On the other hand, as "helper" and "mother," the woman's concerns for "interdependence" and "community" would be an important asset.

"Intellect" and "emotion" are set in opposition, both providing a necessary reaction to the world. For example, consider how the word *torah*[56] emphasizes not raw information, but rather how interrelated knowledge and wisdom shapes it into the important principles and understandings which we sometimes call doctrines or proverbs, and forms the basis of essential instruction. In the Bible, this is the realm of fathers [Psalm 78:5; Ephesians 6:4]:

> Hear, my sons, a father's instruction! Listen, that you may gain understanding! for I give you good insight – do not forsake my *Torah*. ... He taught [root word of *Torah*] me, and said to me: "May my words cling to your heart; keep my commands, and live."   Proverbs 4:1-2, 4

> Fathers, do not provoke [frustrate] your children to wrath, but nurture them up in the training* and admonition of the Lord.   Ephesians 6:4
> *1) the whole training and education of children (which relates to the cultivation of mind and morals, and employs for this purpose now commands and admonitions, now reproof and punishment) It also includes the training and care of the body;   2) whatever in adults also cultivates the soul, esp. by correcting mistakes and curbing passions.   Thayer's Greek Lexicon[57]

Still, this deals with the head, whereas "emotion" connects the heart to experience and adds a different sensitivity in reaction to the world – "groanings" and "sighs" [Romans 8:26] which are beyond words. "Passion," if used in the sense of a deep personal involvement and commitment, would be a good reflection of a God Who would so Love that He would send His only-begotten Son.

"Transcendence" would be in keeping with the head who keeps his eye on *his* Head, "made ... alive together with Christ ... raised ... up together, and made [to] sit together in the heavenly places in Christ Jesus, that in the coming ages He might show the surpassing riches of His grace in kindness toward us in Christ Jesus." [Ephesians 2:5-7]. Meanwhile the woman's "immanence" looks for this reflection coming into Creation, into humanity, giving metaphoric (and real) birth to "Immanuel" – "God with us."

"Culture" is concerned with establishing living conditions, towns, traditions, while the woman as "mother of all living" is mother to the wider picture, to all "nature."

As man "subdues" and "has dominion," he is concerned with "product" – getting the wheat in from the field, making sure the house is sound, getting water to where it is needed. The woman wants the flowers along the way to be appreciated, to enjoy the environment of life, to delight in the "process" of how a child turns into an adult.

"Rules," "rights," "universality," and "impartiality" speak to an orderliness and fairness which reflects God's management of the universe, even to dealing with sin and salvation. Yet laws become detached restraint if there is no "relationship" to give them a heart involvement; "responsibilities" give "rights" a direction and goal; the individual and his/her needs are accounted for, while circumstances are questioned for what contribution they make to given situation (for example, the mother who steals a loaf of bread to feed her starving family).

On the Other Hand

Would that it were so simple!

Think of an army. Throughout history it has been a "community" of "interdependence" (feminine terms) – in fact, "*independence*" (masculine) is very discouraged. This is merely one example of a multitude of situations where caution must be exercised when ascribing traits *exclusively* to one or the other gender. Do men have "passion"? Of course they do, be it sports and games, stamp collecting, woodworking, exploring some unknown or whatever. Do women have "intellect/wisdom"? As a "helper/savior" and "mother," how could they not? A re-read of the capable woman of Proverbs 31:10-31[58] bids us to be careful in pigeon-holing anyone.

We are reminded that in binocular vision, there is very little difference between the eyes; the basic difference is a slight variation in perspective, and yet an utterly necessary one if we are to see in three dimensions. Trying to identify a certain trait as the demarking line between the genders is doomed to failure. Rather, the best way to identify the differences is to look at the stated *reasons* for the *creation* of the man and of the woman as the essential element. Now, within these respective realms of influence, humanity can accomplish its designed purpose of being "the Image of God" to all Creation.

When a parent is single, it is often recommended to involve the child with an opposite gender adult, whether a friend, grandparent, "big brother/sister" or whoever it may be, in order to provide the needed balance for a healthier concept of the human genders. Many single parents really do a good job in their childrearing; still both "male and female" are needed in order to see what Jehovah intended when He designed the human race.

"War"

In the *Stanford Encyclopedia's* article "war" is listed in the "masculine" traits; it is excluded in the comparative list given above because it obviously does not fit with God-reflected traits given to the pre-Fall Adam and Eve. A recent conversation however has caused this to be reconsidered. The fellow mentioned that his daughters seemed from birth to naturally want to cuddle, while the boys, even if they were not given a toy gun, would even use their fingers to simulate one. It just seemed something that is "built into" the males.

On the other hand there is the puzzling omission of "creativity" which should be very prominent in reflecting the Creator. Perhaps "creativity," perverted by selfishness and rebellion, is expressed as "aggression" – or the list's "war." After all, "creativity" can be expressed in achievement and success: for example, if we "create" a cabinet from wood, when the final product stands before us, there is a sense of achievement and success. But in "aggression," its sense of achievement and success is always by exalting one's self at the expense of another person, and even in failure there is the compulsion to blame someone else. In "creativity," ingenuity is used to conceive of something new, whereas with "aggression" the ingenuity is basically used to destroy and control.

No "Turf War"

The masculine and feminine attributes are to reflect God's expression of Himself. Yet infected by the selfishness of "aggression," the man and the woman strive to appear victoriously superior over against the other, as if this were merely a "turf war." The attitude is that the attributes are merely a concoction of culture, or of evolution, as if the field of the "war" is merely something just between humans. Of course, this is the effect of the Fall, where now each has become very conscious of self to the exclusion of any larger picture – or of God's intended reflection.

Such a battle for "superiority" neglects the cosmic responsibility that both have, since the purpose of humanity is: 1) to reveal the Creator; 2) to honor the gender traits as *His*; 3) that the universe, all Creation, yearns to see not "male and female" as isolated individuals, but rather *its beloved Creator reflected in the two of them together*, and 4) the man and the woman represent *not themselves* but ultimately Jesus and His Church. In a "turf war," there is shame over weaknesses, over traits that are not considered powerful enough to push the other down, rather than recognizing how each trait is *Jehovah's* essential way by which making *Himself known through His only "Image"* in this *universe.*

The concern is "the bottom line," where both the man and the woman stand, not battle-bruised raising the flag of victory, but *together* before the One Whom they are to reflect before Creation, before Him Who can say, "Well done, good and faithful servants; you were faithful over a few things, I will set you over many things; enter into the joy of your Master" [Matthew 25:21,23].

An AWOL Gender?

"AWOL" ("absent without leave") is the military's designation for someone who has disappeared without permission. A question arises whether there is an increasing AWOL gender: are men diminishing visibly in many churches?

On one hand this can be as old as Adam's capitulation of his headship to Eve over the matter of the forbidden fruit. Indeed, how often have men "left it to the wife" in regard to the spiritual upbringing of the children? Men have profound influence on their children, whether they realize it or

168

not, whether they want to admit it or not. They cannot escape the responsibility and honor of their involvement in the essential role of head of the family – and this is a *spiritual* office! When the key representative of "the Heavenly Father" is negligent, how significantly does this contribute to our culture's growing disinterest in *Biblical* Christianity.

Does the apathy of many men come from the feeling that they are simply out of place in the Church? Could the culture of the Church – sometimes called "Mother Church" – have become "too feminine" for many men? Do they feel awkward and inept as society itself seems to turn away from the traditional strengths of the man? The "autocratic" leader of the past, perhaps symbolized by Moses or the Pope, are now often looked upon with horror, while the pastor of today is expected to have stronger "feminine" qualities as he "nurtures" his congregation.

Our society (even digital society) seems to increasingly emphasize such things as "community," "connection," and "process" – "being a team-player" – while de-emphasizing "independence," "autonomy," and "product." Less and less in the workplace does a man have a "masculine" distinctiveness.

Forty years ago, there was a strong emphasis on "if it feels right, do it," with a distain for anybody who was "too intellectual" or too rule-bound. This has had effects in the "sexual revolution" and in an increasing tendency to make religion a smorgasbord of appealing doctrines and traditions with no thought as to connection or implications. As schools de-emphasize memory work and learned facts, the actual effect is a reduction of the ability to judge based upon an already acquired fund of information. How do we know when someone is "pulling the wool over our eyes," or how do we judge the accuracy of what we find even on the internet?

Is a void left behind, an emptiness more sensed than describable, where men feel they have little as *men* to contribute to the welfare of the larger group, that they are even redundant, inept, or emasculated? Can a congregation make a man feel that his masculine traits are needed and valued – the masculine traits that are *God's*, given to the man to express a very significant aspect about *His* nature?

Can's and Ought's

This can get messy. The question, "because one can, ought one?" arises. It is the question first encountered in regard to the forbidden fruit of the Tree of Knowledge. Certainly one *can* eat of the fruit, of that there is no question. But *ought* one? "Aye, there's the rub" as Shakespeare once put it.

So, for example, can a woman do the man's tasks? Of course she is capable – again, the Proverbs 31 passage indicates that a woman can indeed be very proficient. Undoubtedly the woman *can* be "just as good as a man." But is the discussion on capability really only a smoke-screen? For example, is God's intent to present the Church as the best well-oiled business model, and/or what perhaps is popular in society – or rather on *how the Creator has chosen to express Himself in humans in all His traits to all Creation*?

The Creator has intentionally made two genders with differences, a definite design and purpose for "the man" and "the woman" within His "Image." "Masculine" and "feminine" are not glibly interchangeable by dismissing the differences which *He* created. The argument is not on personal advancement, but on "advancing" the Creator. Do we submit to – or rebel against – the One Who designed us in this way?

Arguments about equality can merely be veiled selfishness within the struggle for superiority, and a subtle – "cunning"? – rebellion which dismisses the Creator's wisdom, rather than looking for how the both genders are uniquely and purposefully equipped partners *in revealing Him* to the universe. After all, what is it that we are to be about in the final analysis?

170

Part of the call of being God's person in this world is that pleasing ourselves is not our first priority, "for even Christ did not please Himself" [Romans 15:3; also vv 1-2]. St Paul notes in I Corinthians 7:32-34 the tension between pleasing the Lord first, as opposed to pleasing the spouse. Ultimately we are called to "walk worthily of the Lord, into all which is pleasing, bearing fruit in every good work and growing in the knowledge of God" [Colossians 1:10; also Hebrews 13:21]. This does not warrant despising who the Creator made us to be, but rather realizing that we were created for a certain purpose in this *cosmos*, so that it is Jehovah Who is seen not us.

Perhaps this is offensive to some readers, but it is a needed dialogue. After all, how shall we deal with the AWOL gender – their absence may strongly indicate that we are doing something very wrong, and as the saying goes, "they are voting with their feet." Truly, human rebellion is as old as Adam, who was not deceived and who did capitulate to his wife, and it plays its hand in this question. However the real need is to identify *what is God doing in His people because of the genders, not despite them.*

Neither Male Nor Female

> There is neither Jew nor Greek, there is neither slave nor free, there is neither male nor female; for you are all one in Christ Jesus.
>
> Galatians 3:28

What about this passage, where the same St Paul who elsewhere speaks much of "headship," "submission," and the like, also reminds us that "there is neither male nor female"? This verse comes in the middle of his point as to how "in Christ Jesus you are all sons [children] of God, through faith" [v 26]. Truly, no "one is more important" nor will one "be excluded" when it comes to being in Christ Jesus.

But that is dealing with the right to experience salvation, which has nothing to do with God's choice in how, through the balancing of the genders, He reveals Himself in His full "three-dimensions." *The traits are the Lord's,* and ignoring them or dismissing them only diminishes "the Image of God." In fact it is the uniqueness of the differences in each member that makes the *one* Body of Christ [Ephesians 4:4] fulfill its task:

> from Whom the whole Body, fitted together and joined together by what every joint supplies, when each part is working properly, makes bodily growth and upbuilds itself in Love .   Ephesians 4:16

Looking for Jehovah

Can we really say that the infinitesimally small human in the universe has such importance to *all* Creation? Come to think of it, we are the visited planet! Jehovah Himself is intimately involved with humanity from its inception – we are hand-crafted and God-breathed! God the Son Himself became one of us to literally die and rise from the dead for us. The answer is "Yes!"

Too often discussions (or disagreements) in regard to "male and female" stress gender similarity, and ignore any differences as trivial cultural concretions. Yet the presented arguments tend to aimlessly circle around without resolution, based on this or that quality or ability. There will always be outstanding people, and they will be used to confirm or demolish one argument or the other.

However, the anchor is missing which keeps the focus on God's stated purpose for creating humankind at all: "the Image of God" – the Image of the "hidden" God reflected before all Creation and therefore equipped through the Holy Spirit to do that *chiefly within the genders.* Too often we have lost sight of the cosmic significance of this task and are instead focused on very narrow specialties. We must return to the overarching concept of "the

Image of God," not with strident voice to prove our point, but rather with the hushed astonishment that this is really what we are to be about. We do not "sort of fall into" this honor, but rather it is this for which we were uniquely and wonderfully designed, to be within "the Likeness of God's Soul."

This gives us a perspective in regard to our day and in the choices which face us. The judgment is not whether we "can" or are "able" to do this task or that job, but rather "how is *the Creator* being displayed and expressed in this?" Questions about things like mutual "submission" are not merely issues between two people, but rather places where God is to be made visible – made visible *to the universe*. It begins between two people, between husband and wife, and then it expands to parent and child, boss and employee, neighbor and neighbor, human and Creation.

As we become more conscious of the scale of humanity's high privilege – Jehovah being reflected to the universe – then the reality of the *Westminster's Shorter Catechism*'s statement that man's "chief end is to glorify God" begins to take on powerful depth. As Creation finds God's Glory – His "goodness, Covenant relationship, grace, mercy, Steadfast Love, faithfulness, forgiveness, and justice" – reflected through "the Image of God ... male and female," then indeed we shall fulfill a most wonderful "chief end of humankind."

> having your conduct honorable among the Gentiles, that when they speak against you as evildoers, through your good works which they witness, they might glorify God in the day of visitation.   I Peter 2:12

Endnotes

---

[1] For a more in-depth study of this view of Covenant, see: James Lindemann, *Covenant: the Blood is the Life*. (Lethbridge, Alberta: RFLindeman & Son, 2011) – ISBN: paper - 978-0-9877280-0-5; epub - 978-0-9877280-4-3; pdf - 978-0-9877280-7-4; a self-published book, see author's website at www.lindespirit.com for acquiring.

[2] See Trumbull, 25-26, 28; also 36-37. The chief is Itsi, later Ngalyema.

[3] This is THE Love within the Bible – the extraordinary Love which steadfastly holds on to humans and will die even for the adamantly rebellious ones. Hence it is capitalized.

[4] http://www.lyricsondemand.com/z/zagerandevanslyrics/intheyear2525lyrics.html, retrieved 2012-07-17

[5] http://en.wikipedia.org/wiki/In_the_Year_2525, retrieved 2012-07-17

[6] Laird Harris, *et al.*, ed, *Theological Workbook of the Old Testament* [*TWOT*] (Chicago: Moody Press, 1980), Vol I, 951

[7] Harris, *TWOT* Vol I, 404.

[8] Even here, the Land itself does not resist God's agent, but rather "For the land is defiled; therefore I visit the punishment of its iniquity upon it, and the land vomits out its inhabitants" [Leviticus 18:25]. However, should God's agent despise his position, then there is the warning: "lest the land vomit you out also when you defile it, as it vomited out the nations that were before you." [v 26].

[9] Page 13.

[10] There is an interesting side issue here, in response to what is known as "the gap theory." It is thought that in order to explain the fall of Satan and the events surrounding that (for example, the great war in heaven), that there is a "gap" between Genesis 1:1 and verse 2. There are some thoughtful arguments brought forward on this. However, the question needs to be dealt with in regard to whether this has been and will be the only creation God ever has done or will do – note that this is not pursuing the fantasy of parallel universes, but is speaking of entirely new creations. After all, these "sons of God" and "morning stars" could either pre-exist this universe and therefore be the background for the distinctive difference of which the angels are made, or on the other hand, they could also have simply come into being rejoicing and shouting for joy.

[11] Over ninety percent of medicines originated from a plant base, and there are many that have come out of the rainforest environment. What is particularly amazing is that these solutions to the corruption which sin has infected in humanity were so anticipated that the remedies were already in the plant world before humans had sinned.

[12] Many people enjoy their work, but even for them, there come times when under pressure, whether of time or money or whatever, they must continue. During those times, work becomes "toil" – it becomes unpleasant.

[13] Harris, *TWOT,* Vol II, 661

[14] Lindemann, *Covenant, 94.* "*Strong*'s number" refers to the numbering of the Hebrew

words in: James Strong, *Strong's Exhaustive Concordance*.

[15] Lindemann, *Covenant*, 48-49. A endnote reads:

> In 1957, market researcher James Vicary claimed that quickly flashing messages on a movie screen, in Fort Lee, New Jersey, had influenced people to purchase more food and drinks. Vicary coined the term *subliminal advertising* and formed the Subliminal Projection Company based on a six-week test. Vicary claimed that during the presentation of the movie *Picnic* he used a tachistoscope to project the words "Drink Coca-Cola" and "Hungry? Eat popcorn" for 1/3000 of a second at five-second intervals. Vicary asserted that during the test, sales of popcorn and Coke in that New Jersey theater increased 57.8 percent and 18.1 percent respectively. [http://en.wikipedia.org/wiki/Subliminal_message#_ref-5].

[16] page 9

[17] word number 5042; "Kittel'"s *Theological Dictionary of the New Testament* has nothing.

[18] James Lindemann, "He Chose Christiana – Ascension and Mother's Day," http://covenantmusings.lindespirit.com/?p=310

[19] "Feminist Ethics," *Stanford Encyclopedia of Philosophy*, http://plato.stanford.edu/entries/feminism-ethics/, retrieved 2012-07-11

[20] A favorite experience was when reading this passage in a Bible Study, a voice piped up from the back, "See! See! God couldn't create the woman without giving the man a heavy sedative!"

[21] drawn from various sources, one of which is, Matthew Henry's *Commentary on the Whole Bible*, notes on Genesis 3:21–25

[22] Of course, if he is missing a rib, it does not mean all his offspring would now also be minus a rib, the same as if he lost a finger, the offspring would not be short a finger.

[23] There also may be an interesting twist on this from Gary D. Practico and Miles V VanPelt, *Basics of Biblical Hebrew*, Chapter 4 b, http://blakleycreative.com/jtb/BBH/BBH_OH_04.pdf, retrieved 2013-02-03.

> Exceptions to Normal Pluralization. Some singular nouns of one gender take the plural endings of the other gender. For example, the masculine singular noun [ab] (father) takes the feminine plural ending [oth] as in [aboth].

[24] Martin Luther identified that this is the only place in the Bible where the offspring is not referred to as the man's but rather as the woman's Seed, which he interpreted as a prophecy of a virgin birth.

[25] *Christian Digest*, issue #4655, pg: 1067. This account occurs in a few other sources and it appears to have substance, as indicated in the following excerpt of a review of Resa Willis' *Mark and Livy*:

> Willis asserts that Livy tried to "civilize" Clemens by trying to curb his swearing, drinking and smoking, but she makes it clear that Livy soon accustomed herself to her husband's habits. And although during their courtship she planned to turn Clemens into a Christian, she instead followed her husband and fell away from regularly observing the Sabbath during their marriage. Garret Condon

[26] "put in order" – the Greek word is derived from the word *cosmos*.

[27] From the 1662 Church of England's *Book of Common Prayer*

[28] Also Harris, *TWOT*, Vol I, 291:

> But basar [flesh] can be extended to mean 'body' even without any reference to bones. (Num 8:7; II Kgs 4:34; Eccl 2:3, etc.) As such it refers simply to the external form of a person. This is seen as one of the components of the human being, ... they saw the human reality as permeating all the components with the totality being the person.

[29] The excerpt is from an "Instant Messaging" dialogue between the author and a friend, another pastor, Blake Wagner, concerning common-law marriage on 2004-09-23.

[30] Dr Martin H Scharlemann, *The Secret of God's Plan: Studies in Ephesians,* (Saint Louis, Missouri: Concordia Publishing House, 1970), 20.

[31] Fr. John S. Romanides, "Original Sin According to St. Paul" in *St. Vladimir's Seminary Quarterly* Vol. IV, Nos. 1 and 2, 1955-6. the author's website at http://www.romanity.org

[32] James Lindemann, "Marriage: Hosea's Heartgrief, Heart-love, and Heart-hope" - http://covenantmusings.lindespirit.com/?p=377

[33] Also 4:19; 8:22; 9:9; and John 21:19,22.

[34] Online Bible Hebrew Lexicon, in the software: Online Bible Edition; Version 3.00, October 20,2009, 08.26; Canadian copyright 1987-2009 Larry Pierce; 11 Holmwood St. Winterbourne, Ontario, Canada N0B 2V0; http://www.onllinebible.net

[35] Lindemann, "Marriage"

[36] Pages 69-70.

[37] *Helps* Word Studies; copyright © 1987, 2011 by Helps Ministries, Inc; http://concordances.org/greek/2271.htm, retrieved 2012-09-17

[38] Electronic Database. Copyright © 2002, 2003, 2006, 2011 by Biblesoft, Inc. All rights reserved. http://concordances.org/greek/831.htm Retrieved 2012-09-17

[39] Martin Luther, "On The Misuse of the Mass," *Luther's Works*, vol 36, pp 149,150

[40] Some translations preserve the tradition, although the original Greek places Priscilla first.

[41] **Sons of God and Daughters of Men**

A side issue might be mentioned here: there are two passages that have perplexed commentators over the centuries. One is:

> the sons of God saw the daughters of men, that they were beautiful; and they took wives for themselves of all whom they chose. ...The Nephilim [giants] were on the earth in those days, and also afterward, when the sons of God came in to the daughters of men and they bore children to them ...   Genesis 6:2,4

The unanswered question as to what is meant by "the sons of God": In Job [1:6; 2:1; 38:7], the term is understood as the angels; in Daniel 3:25, the fourth person in the fiery furnace "is like a son of God." But if this were the concept in Genesis 6, especially if the Fall had not occurred, then would not the angels have lusted after Eve and her daughters who would have no reason to cover up (which only happened after the Fall)? It would seem strange that God would build into Creation something that would deliberately entice His angels toward breaking His Creation. Even after the Resurrection, when Jesus indicates that we, like the angels of heaven, will "neither marry nor are given in marriage" [Matthew 22:30], it would appear that sexual intercourse is not available between angels, much less between human and angel, not on this earth nor in heaven. Hence, it is most likely that "sons of God" refer to the godly offspring of Adam and Eve, although we really don't know for sure.

The second passage is St Paul's: "For this cause ought the woman to have power on her head because of the angels" [I Corinthians 11:10] – the word that is used, "power," may be understood as the "delegated influence, authority" of the headship to which she is bearing witness by covering her head. But what the reference to the angels means can only be conjectured, and really without a clear basis for the conjecture.

[42] Harris, *TWOT*, Vol II, 697-698

[43] Page 50.

[44] http://en.wikipedia.org/wiki/Single_parent; retrieved 2012-07-18

[45] James Lindemann, "The Magi and Suffering" [http://covenantmusings. lindespirit.com/?p=242]

[46] James Lindemann, "Suffering and the Three Barabbasses" [http://covenantmusings. lindespirit.com/?p=332]

[47] See note 2

[48] Harris, *TWOT*, Vol I, 305-306.

[49] Page 74.

[50] Genesis 18:14 speaks of "his sons–in–law, who had married his daughters," so that it could easily have been that Lot's family itself could have been enough to "save them all."

[51] Harris, *TWOT*, Vol I, 97-98

[52] Harris, *TWOT*, Vol II, 963

[53] Ibid.

[54] http://www.reformed.org/documents/WSC.html; retrieved 2012-12-19

[55] Page 51.

[56] Page 37.

[57] Thayer's Greek Lexicon, (no other information listed on the site), http://biblesuite.com/greek/3809.htm; retrieved 2013-04-10.

[58] Page 132.